COURTING

TRACTOR DATES, MACRA BABIES AND SWIPING RIGHT IN RURAL IRELAND

LIADÁN HYNES

NEW ISLAND

COURTING
First published in 2022 by
New Island Books
Glenshesk House
10 Richview Office Park
Clonskeagh
Dublin D14 V8C4
Republic of Ireland
www.newisland.ie

Paperback ISBN: 978-1-84840-820-3
eBook ISBN: 978-1-84840-821-0

British Library Cataloguing in Publication Data. A CIP catalogue record for this book is available from the British Library.

Set in 12.5 on 17.5 pt Rotation LT Std

Edited by Djinn von Noorden
Front cover illustration by Holly Pereira, hollypereira.com
Cover design and layout: New Island Books
Typeset by JVR Creative India
Printed by ScandBook, Sweden, scandbook.com

New Island Books is a member of Publishing Ireland

10 9 8 7 6 5 4 3 2 1

FSC
www.fsc.org
MIX
Paper from
responsible sources
FSC® C021394

For Kev

and

My sincerest gratitude to everyone who spoke to me for this book, for their time, honesty and energy.

Author's Note

To protect the identity and privacy of some contributors to the book, the author has used pseudonyms where appropriate. In other instances, unique identifying characteristics have been altered in order to protect the privacy of contributors and their loved ones. Some quotes have been edited for clarity. All quotes included in the book are those of the relevant contributors.

Contents

Introduction   1

Part One: The Land
1   The Muddy Matchers   9
2   Tractor Dates   17
3   Macra Babies and Succession   38
4   A Bit of a Change   58
5   Tinder for Farmers and Someone to Talk To   69
6   The Home Place   77

Part Two: Blow-Ins
7   I Was the Last to Know   93
8   Love at First Sight   101
9   Pen Pals   111
10   Go on a Date and Drive for Five Hours   117
11   *Cinegael Paradiso*   127

Part Three: Finding Your Tribe

    12 You're Not Usually My Type   149

    13 Small-Town Life Wasn't for Me   159

    14 I Didn't Want to Be Alone   172

    15 A Tinder Glitch   183

Part Four: Coming Home

    16 How Are *You* Single?   197

    17 I Never Want to Meet People in the Pub   212

    18 I Knew *of* Him   217

    19 Dating Apps Only Work if You Live in a City   223

    20 Somebody from Home   229

    21 A Smaller Pool of People   238

Conclusion   249

Acknowledgements   254

Introduction

In 2018, Tinder released the *Year in Swipe* for the first time, a record of the most noticeable trends on the app that year. And there, just inside the top ten at number nine on the list of cities highest for Tinder activity, was Limerick. Two years later, in early 2020, dating.com listed Ireland as the third most active country in the world when it came to online dating.

My maternal grandparents met at a dance in Cork in the 1930s, when both were in their early twenties. After a long courtship of seven years, they got married and had seven children. My paternal grandparents, who hailed from Galway and Dublin respectively, met at an amateur dramatic society in the 1940s, also while both in their early twenties. They married and had four children. Both sets remained married for the rest of their lives.

My parents met at a house party in the 1970s when they were in their late twenties and early thirties, lived together for several years and eventually married. Unwed cohabiting wasn't especially socially acceptable back then, something they felt particularly after my mother got a teaching job in a convent.

My boyfriend and I connected through Instagram direct messages (DMs), later realising we 'knew of each other' (a phrase that comes up often in interviews for this book, used to indicate a person one feels is safe, for being known, compared to the anonymity of internet dating). We're both single parents, of one child each, in our forties.

How and who we date has changed utterly in Ireland over the past few generations: what age we are when we begin, or return, to trying to find a partner, and where we find them. Online dating has become the main method through which we expect to meet people. In terms of connectivity, the dating applications (apps) have made us accessible to people we would previously never have encountered, something especially relevant for people living in smaller communities. That's the upside. The downside ranges from a culture of disposability in the face of endless choice, to communication that descends on occasion into harassment. Hardly anybody relishes the prospect of the apps, but most people accept their necessity if they want to find a partner.

Our appetite for settling down does not seem to be diminishing. According to 2016 census data, the married population in Ireland increased by 4.9 per cent between 2011 and 2016. That said, remaining married for life is no longer a given. Between 1996 and 2016 the number of people who were divorced grew, as did the number of those who remarried. The proportion of the population that is single increased from 41.1 per cent in 1996 to 43.1 per cent in 2006, then dropped again to 41.1 per cent in 2016.

Interestingly, the largest proportions of single people (aged fifteen or over) were in the cities: Galway was the highest at 53.5 per cent, followed by Dublin at 53.2 per cent and Cork at 51.9 per cent (Leitrim, Roscommon and Meath were the counties with the lowest proportion of single people). The younger the population of a county, the more likely it was to have a high percentage of single people while the older the population, the more married and widowed inhabitants there were. Towns with a population of 10,000 or more people aged fifteen or over had high numbers of singletons.

While married people as a percentage of the population increased between 2011 and 2016 – up from 47.3 per cent to 47.7 per cent – urban areas saw a larger increase than rural ones.

This book looks at the 21st-century dating landscape in rural Ireland: how we meet people, what dating looks like there, how online dating has had an impact on the countryside. Does the place you choose to live inhibit how you will meet someone? Do the traditional ways of meeting a partner – matchmakers, dances, the pub – still provide the most opportunities, or have they been replaced as we all disappear behind a phone screen? And if so, is this a good thing? Is it easier now, or harder, to find a match?

I wanted to look at the modern practicalities of dating in rural Ireland by speaking to as wide a variety of people as possible: people living in farms and on islands, in towns and villages, those who grew up in rural Ireland, some who never left, some who did and then returned, and those who moved there for the first time as an adult.

Dating services aimed specifically at rural communities have long existed. Among these are the annual Lisdoonvarna Matchmaking Festival, built out of our tradition of matchmaking (a process that was originally as much a business proposition as a matter of finding love); matchmaker Mairéad Loughman's The Farmer Wants a Wife events; Macra na Feirme (not officially a matchmaking service, but a voluntary organisation which aims to foster community in rural Ireland, which acts as a place where many couples find love). And alongside them, the social outlets: social dancing, motor meets, investment clubs, sea-swimming. And now, to complement the online era: Muddy Matches, a website that allows you to 'meet rural singles in Ireland'.

All these organisations in their own way acknowledge the specific conditions and challenges involved in trying to meet someone in rural communities.

Isolation – work that can be solitary, lifestyles that revolve around small communities – does not often throw a person in the way of meeting new people. As professional matchmaker Mairead Loughman put it, 'if you put a radius in Tinder of two kilometres, and you're in Dublin, regardless of what age group you're in, you're guaranteed you've got 2–3,000 people to pull out of. If you do that in some parts of rural Ireland, you possibly don't have anybody. And if there are, they're possibly your cousin, or they're your neighbour-down-the-road's daughter who you went to primary school with, and there were only ten kids in the class.'

It's reductive at this stage to suggest that living in a rural setting inherently means living amidst conservative values.

As some of the stories here will show, acceptance of diversity can be abundant. But in smaller communities, just by dint of numbers, anyone outside the 'mainstream' *can* find it harder to find others of a similar mindset. What if you're not straight, not white – what is the experience of dating in smaller, rural communities like then? Conditions such as the experience of being single when it seems like everyone around you is settling down and beginning to have children; chatting on a dating app with someone you may run into professionally in the future; re-entering the dating world, maybe for the first time, after divorce; the value of someone who understands your historical frame of reference, who knows your place and the people from it; the dissonance between those who left and returned and those who always stayed; the tension of loving your home, but knowing it is unlikely to provide you with you a partner? Distance is a further factor, the matter of how you get to know someone when you live counties apart and are not part of each other's day-to-day lives, and the later-in-a-relationship question of who's going to move, given the high unlikelihood that you will meet someone living nearby. What *do* early dates look like if you're driving long stretches to get to each other?

While the starting points were prosaic – how we meet, internet dating and social media and its impact on these things, social outlets, the technicalities of how it all works – so much more came out during my interviews for this book. Conversations about Tinder led to examinations of how being a single woman in a small town has changed, what kind of life one is 'allowed' in those circumstances, and about not wanting children in a society that feels as if it is centred around the family. Speaking to someone about growing up on an island led to a reimagining of the structure of a family. Talking to those in farming revealed matters of vocation, of generational guilt, of a love of a way of life that caused people to leave behind family, friends and place to move to Ireland.

These are stories about knowing what you want from life and finding the person who shares those priorities. In some cases, it turns out it is not a person, but a place that provides. A place which might, at the same time, make it harder to find *your* person. Or even a temporary person.

The stories in this book reveal that in the quest to find a partner, there can be a tension between love and place, that an attachment to place – to the very spot in the world that defines you and where you belong – can make you sacrifice the possibility of meeting someone in favour of the lifestyle you are afforded by the location you have chosen. Or that attachment may be the very thing that identifies exactly who you should be with: a person who understands that lifestyle, that place, and similarly prioritises it.

Part One
The Land

1

The Muddy Matchers

It was 2009 in Borris, County Carlow, and the Muddy Matchers were there to host a speed-dating event, their first foray into the Irish rural dating scene. The Muddy Matchers are Lucy Rand and her sister Emma Royall, founders of the dating website muddymatches.co.uk. The next morning, the pair sat in a local café surrounded by people talking about the previous night – the same people unaware that its instigators sat amongst them. Lucy smiles at the memory. 'It was the chat of the place. They didn't realise that *we* were the Muddy Matchers. It was "shock, horror there's been a speed-dating event".' The event, as it turned out, had been a huge success, it was 'a hoot. We had a really good time doing it.' Lucy smiles now.

Nearly twenty years ago, Lucy and Emma were early adopters in the field of what are referred to as niche dating sites, or more commonly apps which, rather than casting their net at the entirety of the singles market, identify specific communities, tastes and proclivities and cater exclusively to those. These days Muddy Matches is far from being the only one of its kind: name a preference or a community, chances are it has its own dating app. There's Cougar, for mature women; Fitafy, a fitness dating app ('meet active singles and friends who value health and fitness'); Frolo, for single parents; OutdoorLads; Trek Dating; Kippo, the dating app for gamers; Muzz, for Muslim and Arab singles, dating and marriage; Christian Dating Ireland ('calling all single Christians!'); Veggly, vegan and vegetarian dating; Kink D: BDSM, fetish dating; Stache Passions, for moustache lovers; Redhead Dates ('you're sure to find your ginger flame'); Dead Meet, for those who work in the death industry; Bristlr, for beard lovers; Tastebuds, which pairs people in accordance with their musical preferences; and GlutenFreeSingles, for those who practise a gluten-free way of life.

At its most extreme are the invitation-only elite dating apps. Raya, Tinder for celebrities as it is often called, or The League – 'are you told your standards are too high? Keep them that way ... The League, a community designed for the overly ambitious.' The possibility of being turned down upon application to a dating app, a potential further layer of rejection in online dating, has quite the air of what-fresh-hell-is-this to it.

Back when the sisters first launched their business, in the mid-noughties, it was the early days of internet dating, and looking for a partner online was only just on its way to becoming something that was widely considered acceptable, rather than an odd, somewhat embarrassing situation to find oneself in, in some ways an admission of failure. Match.com had launched in 1995, OkCupid in 2004, although it would be years before dating apps made the internet the first port of call for most daters.

LinkedIn had launched in 2003, followed by Facebook in 2004 and Twitter in 2006, all of which had meant that gradually, almost imperceptibly, people were becoming used to the impingement of the internet on their personal space, living parts of their lives online.

Lucy describes the perceptions at the time of online dating as largely something which felt shameful. 'People were starting to talk about it in London. Unfortunately, it *was* kind of seen as freaks and weirdos, or people who were a bit desperate.' Slowly, though, a shift was happening in people's perceptions, she adds.

It was early 2006. The idea for a dating site that appealed specifically to people for whom country living was a priority, and who had a genuine understanding of what that involved, had first come about in the pub. Lucy was living in London when her sister Emma came to visit for the weekend from the countryside. Over drinks, she confided to Lucy about the difficulties of meeting people when living in a rural area. Had she tried online dating? Lucy wondered. She had, but it was full of 'townies'.

Both sisters immediately realised the issue here. They had grown up on a farm in a village. They knew that this could both predispose a person to certain priorities about their way of life, and give them an understanding, insight and yen for rural life that those who grew up differently simply would not comprehend.

'We just kind of figured that everyone knew that that was a thing, it was a niche,' Lucy says. Surely there must be something specifically aimed at people living in the countryside, they thought.

They did some research and quickly realised that, while there were some sites aimed at people living in rural settings, they were very limited in scope. There was a niche within a niche: a specifically equestrian-related dating site, and also a matchmaking site that required a large fee in return for organising only a couple of dates.

Lucy and Emma knew there was a gap: space for something that was a bit of fun, aimed at people who shared a love of the countryside – not just those who were horsey; a space for those who were either already living in or wanted to get back to a rural setting, or who wished to move there for the first time and who were really aware of some of the specific challenges thrown up by farming or rural living; a space where these kinds of people could find each other.

Lucy points to the demanding nature of farming on a person's time. 'Farmers have to cancel dates because they've got trespassers or cows in a ditch. You can't just stop that, it's a way of life, it totally takes over. You're always going to put the animals first, and the farm.'

Then there's the isolation, which living in a rural setting can involve. She tells a story of a former client, a gamekeeper who lived in an especially secluded spot in Scotland. On rare nights out he would meet women and it would often go well – occasionally things might get so far as someone moving in. But within a month or so his partner would be struggling with the long hours he worked, with loneliness, the distance from everything.

'He found it really, really hard to meet someone who could fit in with his lifestyle, and in the end he gave up gamekeeping for a woman because it had happened so many times to him. He never wanted to give up that work, but he wanted that other [domestic] side of his life as well,' Lucy says.

Lucy and Emma didn't imagine Muddy Matches would be a full-time career but decided to 'have a bash at it'. They had been right when they had intuited that there was a desire for a dating forum which placed rural living at its centre. They wanted to create something where people who understood this way of life could find each other. It took off, and the site – yet to be an app (they're a small, family-run business, these things take time, Lucy explains with a grin) – is soon to celebrate its fifteenth year in business. Their oldest Muddy Matches baby is now fourteen.

Not all their members currently live in a rural setting: 'You don't have to live in the countryside to be muddy.' There are younger siblings who didn't inherit the farm and were unable to afford a country property themselves. Now living in town, they are keen to get back to that way of life.

There are 'signed-up townies', those who aspire to a greener way of life and would like to find someone who wants to live off the grid with them. And then there's a few people who like the idea of marrying a farmer, but don't understand the farming way of life: 'not really *actually* that muddy', Lucy smiles wryly. Although the stigma around online dating *was* beginning to slowly shift when they launched the business, it was slower to dissipate in the countryside. This was even more pronounced in rural Ireland than in England, Lucy recalls. That said, soon after they launched their business in Britain, they began receiving emails from Ireland asking why they were not providing the service in this country. 'Why don't you have this in Ireland? We thought, why not?'

At that first event in County Carlow, daters were typically between their thirties and fifties. 'Proper farming community, proper rural people came to that. It was a lot of fun.' At the time of their event, they told the *Irish Times* that they had approximately 2,000 members from the island of Ireland and that, unlike their British members, amongst whom there were slightly more women, membership in Ireland was split equally between men and women. They had chosen Borris because it was one of the 'top ten bachelor hotspots in Ireland' – information gleaned from the 2006 census.

Now everyone dates online, so Muddy Matches has all ages. As the site is subscription-only, it typically attracts people more interested in a relationship than in hook-ups, something they can easily find on the free dating apps. People tend to pay for subscription dating apps for various reasons, for example to avoid the often-brutal nature of the free sites, unsolicited nude pictures, a sense of disposability. 'It's like a cattle mart ... [the men] are showboating, and they think that they can take their pick of women,' one woman I spoke to told me of how she felt about online dating. 'They seem to have a few on the go at the one time.

It's very easy – I could be sitting here watching the TV and having a conversation with four guys if I wanted to, lining them up for each night of the week. That's obviously what people are doing. I felt like I was on a shelf inside of a place, waiting for someone to pick me.'

There is the sense of being more likely to find someone on a site for which you've both paid to be a member. Privacy is also part of the appeal if your tastes run to something you'd rather keep off Facebook and out of the knowledge of those in real life (IRL).

Sometimes, spreading the net more tightly can actually have the inverse effect of revealing someone right under your nose who you might otherwise have missed. One of Lucy's favourite success stories is a couple who had always lived in the same village, always noticed each other from afar, 'maybe they'd seen each other down the pub but not talked.' The village was big enough that they had moved in different circles. It was only through seeing their profiles on Muddy Matches that they realised they were both single and finally got together.

This kind of openness is not always the case; matchmaker and dating specialist Mairead Loughman describes sending a couple from the Tullamore area on a date. The date was taking place elsewhere, and when the woman going on the date asked if it could be moved to Tullamore so there would be less travel, the man, from a small town nearby, immediately refused. 'He was like "definitely not, I'd be afraid somebody would see me". People are more aware of perception, and the people around them and what people think as well.'

She also points to our reflex instinct in Ireland of finding a middle person, to connect a new acquaintance to those we already know. This is not always helpful from a dating perspective. 'So, if you say you're from Mullingar, then they say do you know that family, then you're like, "oh my god, I know her uncle. Eject, eject." There are so many times a guy will come back to me and say, "She's a lovely girl, I don't know if she's the person for me, I would like to have met her again but I know her uncle, I meet him at the mart. I'd just be afraid, say if she took a shine to me, and it didn't work out, sure I'd be the worst in the world. So actually, I'm not going to meet her for a second date." That's rural Ireland for you.'

2

Tractor Dates

Vicki had been out of a relationship for a while when she decided to try Muddy Matches. Now twenty-seven, she was then in her early twenties and, tired of being single, had decided to finally try online dating. 'I started using Tinder, and, like, *all* those rubbishy, weird apps,' Vicki, who is an upbeat, pragmatic kind of a person, says with a roll of her eyes. She tried Bumble and Plenty of Fish as well. 'That was my first time using them and I just met weirdos.'

She found herself, 'talking to people who never in a million *years* would you think about meeting in real life, because they were just weird. There were a couple of people who I went on dates with, and I just thought, No. No, not for me. Your pictures were lovely, but your personality is not what I'm looking for, thank you very much,' she adds briskly.

Vicki grew up in Essex in England, 'literally in the middle of town. What I would class as a normal upbringing,

17

whereas I'm sure the guys here would class it as an abnormal upbringing,' she laughs, waving a hand around at the farm where she now lives.

When she was five, she took up ballet lessons. At the time, her grandfather, who had always loved animals, a trait he has passed on to his granddaughter, suggested she also try horse riding. Her mother told her she wasn't paying for both, so Vicki had to choose. She picked horse riding and 'never looked back'.

Now she cannot remember a time when she didn't think she would work with horses. She studied equine training and management at university, going on afterwards to work on the farm of a National Trust stately home. The internet dating was not going well when she came across Muddy Matches through an ad for the site on Facebook. 'It piqued my interest, an online dating website, specifically for farmers-slash-outdoorsy people.'

The thought of paying a subscription fee initially put her off, however, and she decided to carry on with 'crappy dates, meeting weirdos' for a little longer. Nothing improved, and eventually Vicki thought, 'Sod it. I'm going to pay for one month's subscription, and I might meet somebody amazing.'

And she did. Within three days she had met her now boyfriend, Stephen.

'My lifestyle didn't really fit with a *normal* person's lifestyle, someone who did a nine-to-five job in an office,' Vicki explains. 'I didn't have enough in common with people I was meeting.' When she would mention things like staying late at work to wait for the vet to attend to a sick animal, they would look at her blankly and say, 'It's five o'clock, go home.'

There's a vocational element to how Vicki views her work – it and the rest of life are in communion with each other rather than being independent entities. It's a sensibility that is common in farming, in that it is not just a job but a way of life. There is good and bad within this – a life spent so much in nature, but also an acceptance of the at times all-consuming demands of farming life; a love for the pace of it, relentless on occasion, but also less gruelling in many ways than more urban-based work.

For Vicki, the importance of an existence which prioritised the outdoors meant there was too much of a disconnect between her and the men she met on the regular apps she had been trying before joining Muddy Matches. It's not that you have to be with someone who is *exactly* the same as you, she is quick to add. But some things are too big, too important, to not have a mutual interest in and understanding of.

'Stephen and myself are incredibly different people, but the thing that we have in common is the love for farming and the outdoors and animals. And that is more important. I would much rather have someone ... who is different than me, but who gets the lifestyle, than have someone who has all the exact same hobbies and interests as me but doesn't like farming and animals.'

When they first connected on Muddy Matches, Stephen was living about forty minutes away, working on a large arable farm where he had been employed for three years on the tractors. Does she remember what it was that first struck her about him?

She grins. 'He's very pretty. I know it sounds like it should be so much deeper because the site is more specific,

19

but you're still meeting somebody based on their photograph, and there's still that sort of shallowness of "yes, this person is pretty, let's find out more about them".'

Vicki messaged first: Stephen had also just signed up to the site. Numbers were soon exchanged and they began talking on WhatsApp. After about a week a date was arranged. He had organised bowling, which impressed her, 'I think it's the only thing he has booked in our entire time together, but it was enough,' she laughs.

What happened next was what made this date so different from all the others. 'At the end of the bowling I said to him, "We need to go somewhere else, let's go to a pub or do something." I didn't want it to end. All the other dates, you get to the end of them and you're like, oh thank *god*, I can go home again now – I don't have to keep forcing the conversation.'

With Stephen she thought, no, I'm not done yet, you need to stay. Happily, he felt the same.

They went on five dates in the space of a week. It was like finding someone who understood exactly the thing that was most important to her, Vicki recalls. 'We were having those conversations like, "oh my god I know what you mean". Or he'd tell a story and I'd be like, "almost exactly the same thing happened to me, listen to my version of it".'

None of Vicki's family or friends is in farming, so she relished finding someone who had the same appreciation as she did. 'And he is cracking. He's always been awesome. I think I knew pretty quickly … yeah, you'll do.'

The 'talk' – whereby two people agree that they will no longer speak to anyone else on dating apps – happens at various stages but for Vicki and Stephen it came quite quickly. 'I think both of us had been still talking to a few other people on the website, because you go on so many rubbish dates that you kind of think it's pointless not talking to anybody else. Quite quickly we had the conversation of "are you still talking to people on the website or not?",' she smiles shyly. 'And you kind of go, "I'm not if you're not."'

It was February when they met and by the end of the summer they were living together. This acceleration in the progress of their relationship was mainly because of Stephen's job, and the all-consuming pace of farming at certain seasons. Come the harvest, if she hadn't 'put the effort in' she would never have seen him, so long were his hours. Some nights Stephen could be out working on the tractor until three, come home, get some sleep and then be back out again by eight in the morning. It's not a timetable that leaves much room for conventional dating. Vicki was unperturbed by this.

'There's nowhere in that time where you can say "oh right, now we're going for a date". And I totally got that. That's the life, that's what you expect.'

To combat this, they came up with a concept that worked around, or rather with, Stephen's work. Tractor dates. If Stephen couldn't take time off work to meet Vicki, she would simply go to his place of work: the field, where she would sit up in the tractor with Stephen.

'They have periods of time where the job has to get done by a certain date. But you can't start the job until a certain time, so everything has to happen in the space of two weeks. If I didn't go and sit up in the tractor for a couple of hours, I wasn't going to see him.'

Your evenings no longer consist of sitting in front of the TV, you have to accept that, Vicki says. Instead, it's 'sitting in a tractor. Because otherwise you won't get to spend time with the person'.

Dates on the farm get a mixed reaction. One woman I spoke to recounted in tones of can-you-believe-it how she was once invited to the milking parlour on a date. Another told me proudly of how her partner, also a farmer, had come to the farm she worked on for their date, a rare reversion in the gender balance of how these things tend to play out, she felt. Vicki loved tractor dates and looks a shade wistful when she talks about them and how she quite misses them. 'There'd be times when you'd be like, "oh this is such a pain," but on the whole I used to really love it.'

Vicki would bring her dog Wispa and food, maybe a pizza, and drive to a field where Stephen was working. Her favourite tractor dates were those on weekend mornings rather than weekday evenings, as it would be bright and she could spend the entire day with Stephen, driving up and down the field, chatting, listening to music.

Every so often Vicki would get out and take Wispa for a few laps around the edge of the field while Stephen kept the tractor going up and down. At lunchtime, she would head into town for supplies.

'It would turn into a whole-day kind of thing, which I think we both kind of enjoyed, because he enjoyed the company and I enjoyed getting to spend time with him and being out and about. At the beginning of our relationship, I was much less farmy, so for me it was the novelty of it. It did very quickly become more commonplace and less exciting and new. Whereas at the start it was definitely "ooooh, look how big the tractor is, and I get to sit in it",' she laughs.

Initially, Stephen wasn't sure if Vicki would stay the course, or if the extreme nature of his working hours would put her off. He confided later that he thought he really liked her, but he'd see what happened come spring. 'We got through spring, and he was like, "oh this is great, but I'm sure she'll leave by harvest, because harvest is mental".' When we got through harvest, I think he was a bit like, "huh, maybe she's not leaving",' she smiles.

Two years after they met, both Vicki and Stephen began to feel that it was time to look for new jobs. Vicki had always known that someday Stephen would want to move home to Ireland where his family has a farm in Dunmanway, a market town in the west of Cork most famous for being the birthplace of the Gaelic football player Sam Maguire, which, according to the 2016 census, had a population of 1,655.

There were many conversations between Vicki and Stephen about the move. They both felt the relationship had a future. Stephen didn't have an ownership stake in the family farm but was still personally invested in it. Vicki saw her future with this man, that they would get married and have a family. That sense of certainty about the relationship helped in contemplating a move to Ireland, and to a relatively isolated setting where she knew no one.

Living in a rural setting means you are quite likely to meet someone living some distance away, rather than nearby in your community. Simple logistics, such as a bigger community like those found in urban areas, means more choice nearby. The fact that, if things become serious one person in the relationship will have to move, is very often built into the expectations from the outset of dating.

The smaller the community, the more conscious of this possibility the couple is. When one person is a farmer, their location, or the location of the family farm, is an immovable feast and tends to be the deciding factor as to where the couple will end up. 'It was easier for me to compromise my life than it was for him to compromise his. Everyone has their own personal little drama. Everybody has something that they've gone, "I've given up that for this, or we're making this decision for that reason." And this was ours,' Vicki says matter-of-factly.

These decisions aren't always made with such autonomy. One woman I spoke to described her experience of moving with her then boyfriend, now husband, thirty years ago, from England to his family farm in the south of Ireland, thereby 'giving up town life'.

Both she and her Irish partner had jobs in England and were enjoying life there but, she said, 'he was getting constant phone calls from his mother, saying that they couldn't run the farm without him. It was quite early in our relationship, but there was no other option but for me to pack up everything and move over.' Doing so meant leaving her family, friends and social life behind, she says. Louise had no experience of farming, having grown up in a city. Then in her early twenties, she found herself living in her boyfriend's family home and working on the family farm. 'I just got stuck straight into everything that was going on over there. I would have started to milk even though there was no farming in my background at all. My dad used to laugh at me, because I always used to shop in Next, and I always had to have a new outfit for going out every Friday night. He'd say, "Look at her, she used to be so la-de-da." I was never la-de-da,' she adds with a smile.

Getting out on the farm did help with the homesickness, and in dealing with her challenging mother-in-law-to-be. 'She used to bash on the ceiling with the brush on a Sunday morning to tell us to get up and go and do the milking. You might have just got in [from a night out].'

Even though her husband was not the eldest son, he had been the one involved in the running of the farm from a young age, unlike his older brother who had no interest. They had been promised the farm if they returned from England but, once in Ireland, this failed to materialise for years. 'That was the carrot that was dangled in front of us all the time.

Their work on the farm was not financially remunerated: 'It was more or less your board and lodgings that you're working for. It's your duty to do this because you're being kept. Sometimes you'd have to ask for a few pound on a Saturday night.

'You'd get out for a quick spin around on a Sunday afternoon. 'Cause she'd woken us, we'd do the morning milking, and then we'd to be back to do the evening milking. So really all you had as a young couple was just a few hours on a Sunday afternoon spinning about. You had to make sure you were back on time.'

25

Vicki's decision to move to her partner's family farm in Ireland was entirely different, being made free of any guilt and involving a lifestyle she actively pursued. Eventually she and Stephen decided to give living in Ireland a go, moving in December 2020.

'I know the answer should be, oh yeah it was really hard. But actually, the decision-making was really easy. I'd rather do something and think, *I wish I hadn't done that*, than not do it and always wonder.' It was the aftermath that was trickier than she expected.

Before moving, Vicki had visited Stephen's family home three times, bringing her parents on one occasion. It wasn't necessarily a foregone conclusion that they would live in his parents' home. They discussed the possibility of getting their own place. It was during these conversations that Stephen's parents offered to convert the loft in their house for the couple.

The family home is located on Stephen's uncle's dairy farm. 'They've got about sixty-eight milking cows, it's about eighty-six acres, with another twenty-four or so that are rented. So it's quite a small dairy farm, but for around here, it's probably average-ish size,' Vicki says.

It is very much a family-operated farm. Stephen's uncle and his brother run it together in a farm partnership :an agreement where two farmers decide to work together to share resources, usually between two family members on the same farm, intra-family, but occasionally intra-farm, where two farms will join forces for economies of scale, to have a shared workload and improve the work-life balance.

The majority in Ireland are family-farm partnerships. Initially in a farm partnership, the father or the mother still owns the land, the young person is coming in as a partner in the business but they do not own the land. Typically, though not always, a farm partnership registered with the Department of Agriculture will lead to succession.

Originally, Stephen, the elder of the two brothers, was to go into partnership, but as he stayed longer than expected in the UK it passed to his younger brother. The farm can support one full income, and a small amount for his brother. Stephen's uncle is the only one who doesn't have any other employment, although everyone in the family works to some extent or another on the farm. 'But not a single one of us is doing it for the money. We're all doing it because it's the life and that's what we like. It is what it is,' Vicki says, going on to describe a sort of bartering mentality, where her horses live for free on the farm and she works there in return.

Stephen has a job on a farm down the road, across the valley on the next hill, Vicki says, pointing from their living-room window set into the sloped roof. Their home is surrounded by hills and the area is sometimes referred to as 'the gateway to the mountains'. He works there mornings and evenings and, in the afternoon, puts in a shift on the family farm.

In part, moving to Ireland was difficult because of lockdown. It wasn't the first time Vicki had moved. She had done so in England, therefore did have some idea of what to expect. This time, however, she found that all the things she would normally do to set up a life for herself in the new place – joining clubs, exercise classes – were unavailable to her. She had no job, no family, no friends. And Vicki is a very social, engaged type of person, the kind you would imagine makes new friends easily. So she struggled, both with the simple lack of things to do, but also the sense of being so dependent on her partner for a life.

Then there was the culture shock. 'I think the most challenging thing was how different the people are compared to the people that I'm used to.' She didn't expect it. 'Everyone is so friendly and chatty to each other. It was very weird to begin with and I struggled with it. But I actually kind of like it now.' She has made her peace with the fact that shopping is a social activity that can take hours.

'I'm used to it now, but when I first came over, I went into SuperValu, and I remember walking round it and saying to Stephen, this feels so foreign. It was just set up so differently to how an English shop was set up. Considering that England is literally right next door, and we're not far away, it is so different, and I think that was a bit of a shock when we first moved over. I was expecting it to be quite similar. And it really isn't. But it's okay. Once you get your head around, well, you're not living in England any more so why would it be the same?'

The 2016 census showed a small number of local people whose birthplace was the UK. West Cork has long seen an influx of people moving to the area from other countries. Historian Dr Richard Butler, Director of Research at Mary Immaculate College, Limerick, lives in west Cork. 'West Cork and west Kerry in particular were places which historically had huge amounts of emigration outwards. People left to go abroad, because there were big families, and poor farms, and quite poor land in many cases. And very few opportunities.'

The mid-sixties saw the population in west Cork bottom out to a historical low in modern times. 'It's a time when land prices are really cheap, and there are lots of old farmhouses that are being abandoned in many cases. And it's possible for people who are looking for an alternative lifestyle to come into west Cork, and to buy up old farmhouses, maybe with some land. West Cork is best known for having a community of people that moved from abroad who would be seen by some as hippies or alternatives. People that want to live a different kind of lifestyle away from cities, away from the busy life, away from technology is some cases. They want to live in the countryside, grow their own food, live with nature.'

Immigration to the area was especially high in the 1970s, eighties and nineties, not just with English people but many Dutch and Germans also. 'Certain places in west Cork became known as places where there was a very international community. That in itself drew more people to come in and join them. You tend to get clustering. In the same way that when Irish people went to Kilburn back in the day, more Irish people would also go to Kilburn. That kept going until the Celtic Tiger years, when house prices and land prices went up to the point that it was no longer cheap.'

When I visit Vicki at home on the farm, it's almost eight months since she moved to Cork, and it's only now that she is slowly beginning to feel properly settled. The previous months had been difficult, to the point where her mental health had suffered.

'I am quite a happy, good-outlook-on-life kind of person. I struggled with maintaining that. You get to a point where you're just a little bit like, "this isn't natural now. I'm faking the fact that I'm happy, and I'm now trying really hard to put a happy face on for everything."'

This was inevitable with such a big move, she feels, trying to rush her acclimatisation would not have helped. These things need to happen naturally and organically.

Living with Stephen's parents at first, who have been 'amazing', meant an added layer of pressure to disguise when she was feeling down. Where she could show Stephen how she was feeling, she didn't want his parents to think she was ungrateful for their hospitality, or that she didn't like living in their home.

Vicki strikes me as someone who is energised by being around other people. Suddenly there was no one but her partner and his family. 'It was definitely hard, especially to begin with. That's a lie – not even to begin with, I think it has been hard for a long time. The fact that the only people I was really seeing were Stephen and his family [was challenging]. The odd occasion when one of the neighbours would pop over to say 'hi', or if we would be doing some work out in a field somewhere and we were near somebody else's house, and they'd just pop over the wall to have a chat, I'd literally be finding myself ten times happier because I'd had a conversation with somebody different.'

She assumed that things would change when they came out of lockdown, but as restrictions lifted Vicki began to realise that maybe it wasn't just Covid-19 stopping her from making inroads and creating a life for herself beyond the farm, in the way she might normally do in a new place, that this might be the tenor of her new place, the rhythm of life there.

'I kept saying, "When we're out of lockdown I'll do this, or that." Now we're out of lockdown I've started looking for things to do, and there's not actually that much *to* do. Because everybody here is a farmer, they don't have the time to do other stuff. I don't think lockdown would have made a single bit of difference to my experience of moving over. I probably would have tried a little bit harder to join activities only to find that they weren't there to join.'

Gabriela Meade Diaz moved to a small village in Mayo in 2019. Like Vicki, she moved to be near her partner. The women's experiences mirror each other's in many ways. Originally from Mexico, Gabriela was living in Dublin when she met her boyfriend through Tinder. Two months into seeing each other he told her he was moving home to County Mayo, to Claremorris, to start his own business.

At first, they did long distance, but its appeal was finite. 'That went well for a year, but then I know myself. I told him "this is not a permanent solution". Gabriela, who is thirty-three, moved to Mayo Abbey, a small village near Claremorris, in 2019. The couple are now living in a rented property. (They were lucky, she explains. Rental properties in the area are not plentiful. Several couples had looked at the house but the landlady gave it to them because Gabriela's partner's family is from the area. 'Here everybody asks you who you are related to. And if you are not related to someone, it's a bit like, "Who are you? What are you doing here?"')

31

Just like Vicki, she found the first few months after moving difficult. 'I'm a city girl. I used to live in Mexico City, and then Dublin. I'm used to being connected. You walk out on the street, there's a bus, and you can go to shops.' Instead, without an Irish driving licence, she was reliant on her partner for lifts. Like Vicki, she bridled at the curtailing of her independence. (Vicki described to me Stephen's attempts to set her up on a friend date with a woman who is also into horses. 'I can make my own friends,' she'd huffed.)

'That drove me *crazy*,' Gabriela says of her temporary inability to drive. 'The fact that I had to tell him "oh I need to go to the shops" and he was like "okay, I can do it at this time", because he was working.'

She knew no one and without a job and the introductions that naturally provides, she struggled to create connections in her new setting. It took a year to find employment and, in the end, her boyfriend's mother arranged an interview in the pharmaceutical company in Castlebar where she herself had worked. She began her new role just as the pandemic started.

'I needed that, because I was very isolated before. It hasn't been easy at all. You start realising how much you depend on someone, and I've always been very independent. Now I've been discovering that my favourite things I do are kind of based on what he likes. Because I am in his world. I'm like no, I cannot be doing this. It's not healthy. Everybody needs their own life, away from the partner.'

She found it hard to make friends in work – in part this was down to Covid-19, and the lack of socialising it allowed for. She also sensed an attitude on the part of some, though not all, of her Irish co-workers, that they already have their circle of friends. 'It's very difficult for them to open up again and bring someone in. Especially after your thirties, maybe it's easier for younger people. So for example in work, the people that I gather with are mainly foreigners.'

The move was initially tougher than Gabriela had expected. Just like Vicki, she estimates it took a year to really settle in the new life, but she is 'perfectly happy now'. Having adapted to the slower pace, she relishes the quiet, the lower stress levels, the immersion in nature, the ability to rent an entire house with a sizeable garden for what in Dublin got her a small room in a shared house.

'At this stage in life I like this place, the slow pace.'

Eight months into her move, Vicki says she sees her future in Dunmanway, but you get the sense that that is very much because this is where Stephen is, rather than because she has any attachment to the place or has managed to start a life for herself there independent of her relationship. She has a job on a nearby dairy farm – she did an online course before moving to Ireland 'to try and learn about Stephen's world'. And she loves it: the slice of autonomy has made a huge difference. 'I'm milking [cows] for this lovely couple. That is probably one of the things about here, everybody is lovely. It's so different to where I'm from in that people talk to each other and know each other. It's nice having my own responsibility again, and my own little world.'

When it came to looking for work, a little like the tractor dates, Stephen's work schedule and fitting around that was a priority. She doesn't mind. 'The only reason I'm here is for him. If I get a job that means I'm not seeing him [then] what's the point in being here?'

The milking job twenty minutes away from their home is perfect, as she works in the mornings and evenings. She and Stephen will have lunch together, then hang out – they're big *Home and Away* fans, she laughs. Vicki is a little concerned the job is not going to offer her the possibility for expansion in the long term, and doesn't seem overly hopeful about the prospect of finding something that will. She's *hoping* the role she is in will let her get more involved, but the future feels full of unknowns, and that is hard. Her future is here, but quite what the actual nuts and bolts of that future will look like are uncertain.

I ask her about the opportunities she feels the area will afford her for a career that remains engaging, and she bursts out laughing, then shakes her head ruefully.

'I have put a *lot* of energy into trying *really* hard to not think about that question,' she says a little uneasily, and it feels for a moment as if I've reminded her of something she's been doing her best to ignore. 'It's really difficult, because as much as right now I'm really loving what I'm doing, I'm very aware that the job I had before stretched me a lot more and gave me a lot more opportunities. And I need that, I need something that's challenging.'

We speak again several months later – it's now just over a year since Vicki moved to Ireland. She's beaming. Their loft apartment is well underway: she proudly shows me her new kitchen, which has just been installed. Her own projects are thriving: she has two Shire horses and two dogs she wants to breed. The job has come good, it looks like there is room for more involvement. Her understanding of her new place has deepened immensely, too. 'Just over a year into it now, and I think I've got there. It's taken months and months and months to get my head around the different pace, the different way that things are done.'

Vicky now has an understanding of the way of life around her she didn't have before. 'Like the different priorities. When I first moved over, it would be ten, eleven, twelve o'clock at night, and the boys would still be up at the farm. And I'd be sitting here like, "are you kidding? You could do this tomorrow during the day. This doesn't have to happen now." I didn't get it. Whereas now I totally get that you do need to do that now. Because yes, you would have time to do it tomorrow, but there's seventy other things you need to do then. If you don't get this done today, it just means tomorrow's going to go on even longer.' You can sense the respect in her tone for what goes into the running of the farm.

She is more able to appreciate some of the sacrifices that Stephen made when they first moved over. 'At the time I don't think I fully registered it, because I was feeling a bit crappy, lonely and stressed out and not particularly happy for a while. He would go out of his way to say, "we're going to go out for the day, I'm not going to farm this afternoon, we're going to go and do whatever." I appreciated it but thought at the same time this should just be normal. You shouldn't have to be going out of your way to spend time with me. Now I know there's a hell of a lot of effort that he put into that, to make sure that he still had time for me as well. I needed time to realise how life worked here.'

Vicki and Stephen see less of each other now than they did when they lived in England. 'And I didn't see a lot of him when we were living in England,' she laughs. 'But I think what has changed it though is that because he's a lot happier, and a lot more enjoying life, the time that we do get to spend together is a lot nicer. Because he's on top form, you know. And now that I'm settled, and I've acclimatised myself, I'm really quite enjoying life here too. So when we do get time to spend together, it's fun, it's nice, we're both having a good time.'

She's carved out a niche for herself, she explains proudly. 'I've got these things that are mine to spend time with. I'm not having to just rely on Stephen for entertainment. I don't feel any more like I'm counting down the time until he's back from work. Now there'll be times when he'll text me at lunchtime saying he's on his way home, and I'll be like, "oh, I'm not ready. I'm still busy."'

That's how life should be, she adds, balanced, not one person overly dependent on the other. 'It's got to that point where we're both busy and we've got stuff on, and that's what's made me feel a lot more settled and a lot more together with living here now, because I'm just as busy as he is.'

Their social life is still a work in progress. 'Everybody goes out so bloody late here. Like, they start at ten. Because everybody has to milk before they can go out. The couple of times we came over and visited here before moving, we'd be going out with his friends, and I'd be ready at say seven. "Right, let's go,"' she laughs.

She has adjusted her expectations. 'Rather than trying to make new friends, it's been more adapting to how I see my old friends. We're a hotel for the summer.' Stephen's friends are in farming as well, so finding the time to meet up can be difficult. 'The couples that I know of through Stephen's friends met at school and they're still together. If you didn't meet at school, I've no idea how you meet people. Stephen says not only had he not moved to England, but had he not gone online dating, he wouldn't have met me. Because he didn't have the time.'

Will they stay?

Vicki grins. 'Yeah, I think so. I think we're settled enough here, and we've got a little plan, and we're happy here now.'

3

Macra Babies and Succession

Although they only know each other vaguely through the agri-influencer community, Sophie and Mark have several things in common. Both are twenty-three, and while neither is the eldest sibling in their family, each will inherit their family farms. In Sophie's case, by next year she will have full responsibility for and ownership of the family farm she grew up on in Virginia, County Cavan, where she lives with her parents. It will mean shouldering financial and logistical responsibility for the enterprise, a dairy farm of about fifty acres with 'forty cows at the moment, but I think it will be more as we go along. I am young, and I am a girl; two of the things that don't normally happen when taking over a farm'. Sophie acknowledges these unique circumstances as we walk uphill in the field behind the family home, the silhouette of her mother at a window behind us.

People are surprised to hear that she has an older brother, she says, and that he is not the one taking over.

'They ask, what's your brother doing? We would often be asked why he isn't farming, seeing as he's the brother.'

Sophie wasn't always sure she wanted to take this path. Her desire to go into farming waxed and waned over the years. Growing up she knew she wanted to do *something* in relation to animals, but in primary school, in class with kids doing other things, she temporarily lost interest in farming. It returned in secondary school, where she was surrounded by 'like-minded people', and she went on to study agriculture and animal science in England. It was this move that meant it was assumed at home that she would go into farming.

'Whenever I finished college I was asked, "when would you like to?" We didn't really sit down to talk about it, but we did involve the whole family, just so that everyone was aware.'

Of going into succession, she says, 'I think it's very important to not make a big deal over it. A lot of families can get into fights and stuff about handing over the farm, because it can be a big deal. I think it's important to be open about it.'

Gordon Peppard, a collaborative farming specialist with Teagasc (the semi-state authority responsible for research and development, training and advisory services in the agri-food sector), explains this most delicate of farming matters, which can, in the worst circumstances, give rise to tragedy. 'Succession is the planned route for the handover of the management of a business or a farm. It is distinct from inheritance, which is the legal transfer, or the sign-ing-over of the land, putting the land into the name of

the young person and into their ownership. I would seg-
regate succession out as the management of the business,
whereas inheritance is the actual physical taking over
of the ownership of the land and the assets.' Succession
involves the decision of how the farm is passed from generation to generation.

Who actually runs the business is a sensitive matter, he
explains. 'Farming is a way of life. A lot of farmers never retire.
What generally happens is that as the wheel turns, instead of
an eighty–twenty split of the labour that reverses, and over
time the young person ends up with a bigger share, and the
older farmer is weaned off, we'll say. What happens in many
farms is the father or the mother might step back, but they
don't step away. They're still there in a guiding capacity. They
have knowledge and experience of the land and the farm
over maybe fifty, sixty, seventy years. That shouldn't be disre-
garded. So they're there in a mentoring capacity. They may be
there to do odd jobs, small jobs, jobs that need two people.'

Succession on farms can be a very taboo subject in
Irish agriculture. Gordon describes the reluctance at times
on the part of parents to broach this potentially awkward
topic. 'There's a lot of fear amongst parents that they don't
genuinely know how to be fair. They have a farm asset, they
see that *they* needed that full farm to make enough of an
income to rear the family, they're afraid that if they split
it up between their children it won't be viable to anyone.
However, if they give it to one person they're giving them
a big asset, and they're leaving the others with no asset. I
think in a lot of cases they want to be fair but they don't
know how to be fair, so they avoid it.

'In a lot of scenarios, most siblings actually know who's going to get the farm, or they know who should get it, who is the right fit for the farm. I think what the icebreaker is really is if the parents actually sit down around the able and say, "look, we'd love to be able to give you all the farm, but we obviously can't. We feel that Tommy is the right person for it." It's to be involved in the discussion and be told – that's important to the siblings.'

Mark, who lives in Kilkenny, always knew he wanted to go into farming. 'It is my passion,' he says, explaining that when his oldest sister was in sixth year and deciding what she would study in college, someone said to the then twelve-year-old boy in passing, 'Mark what do you think you'll study?' He picked dairy business in UCD, then a new course. Years later, he would graduate with this degree.

For the time being, Mark works on the family farm with his parents. When his father, and then Mark himself, were teenagers, each became involved in big decisions around the family farms. His father, now in his fifties, was sixteen when he suggested to his parents that they sell their land in Cork and buy instead in Kilkenny.

Mark's grandmother, 'a driving force', he says, had realised that the farm they owned in Cork was not large enough to provide a living for her two eldest sons, both of whom wanted to farm. The family had begun looking for a bigger farm. It was Mark's father, the then sixteen-year-old second son, who had spotted the difference in the price of the land and suggested they look to Kilkenny. 'There wasn't a lot of opportunity to get a farm that was much bigger down in Cork. The land wasn't as good up here, so you could get twice the amount for the same money. They decided to go with that.'

In 1979 they bought a working farm in Callan, County Kilkenny, quite small when they arrived, but they have added to it over the years so that now, including the land they have leased, they have 445 acres and 400 cows. It's where Mark and his two older sisters grew up with their parents and his grandparents.

In 2013 the farm next door came up for sale. Mark was then fifteen but, like his father had been years before, he was involved in the discussions around whether the family would purchase the land. 'You know, there wasn't much point in us buying the farm if I didn't want to work. Because I was going to be the one farming here in the future. So I would have been very involved in decisions like that. I was *glad* to be involved, as much as anything. When I was younger, I was either in school, I was playing sport, or I was at home. That was about it. Through the weekends and in the summer, I'd always be here at home, working every day.'

Having recently finished college he is home farming full time. The house, which dates from the early seventeenth century, is an elegant old property with large sash windows and a slate-clad wall to the rear. He meets me in the large court-yard at the back of the house and brings me through to the kitchen, where a Sheila Maid clothes airer hangs from the ceiling over the Aga. A large wooden dresser is full of Nicholas Mosse crockery. It's a hard house to heat, Mark says, adding that this room is where the family spends most of its time. The kitchen's walls are about three feet thick and look out onto an old walled garden. He busies himself making tea, organising a plate of cake and biscuits, a jug of unpasteurised milk from the farm. He is an extremely polite person – when I ask, ridiculously, if there are any hand-milking parlours left in Ireland, his face barely twitches until I say, 'you're trying not to laugh at me aren't you?' at which he allows himself a grin.

He shows me around the farm after tea, proudly leading me through the sizeable milking parlour they put in themselves and several barns out the back, pointing to a newer wing at the rear of the house where he sleeps.

From the point of view of inheritance, it's always been about the farm supporting all three of the siblings, giving them all equal opportunities, something a large farm can afford to do. The family's succession plan – that Mark would be the one to take over the farm – was something that was always known amongst all the siblings. 'Because it was really progressive and open, it wasn't a matter of sitting down and it being discussed too much,' he says of the approach his parents have taken. 'I suppose everyone knew what was going to happen. We knew I wanted to go into farming, we knew my sisters didn't want to go into farming. Because it was a more open, ongoing conversation, there wasn't a need to sit down and go through it all.'

He knows this isn't always the case. 'Within agriculture, succession is a big problem because it can be quite delayed, and people don't talk about it – they're afraid to. I suppose maybe for older people, they feel that they don't want to let go of the farm. They may have only got the farm themselves when they were sixty, so they want to keep it a little bit before they hand it down again,'

On occasion, the issue can be between siblings. I spoke to one family where the eldest brother had moved abroad and shown no interest in the family farm for years, while the younger had stayed and run the farm. Years later the eldest returned, having decided he wanted to claim what he saw as his rightful inheritance. 'He thought he could come back and because he was the eldest son, he automatically thought it was going to be his. His parents had always treated him like the prodigal son. It was handled very badly. They were very vague for some time to both sides about it.'

There was a row, over thirty years ago, and the two brothers haven't spoken since. Not uncommon, this farmer added. 'Me and Dad work really well as a team,' Mark says, 'so it was never so much of "oh I'm handing this over to you now", it's always just working together.' There's something lovely about being happy to follow in the footsteps of the life you grew up in. There's also something all-consuming about being handed this entire project, though, not swerving into another way of life and trying out different jobs in your twenties, or moving about, into the path of new people.

Her workload doesn't leave much space for a social life at the moment, Sophie says. 'If you do go out, you're tired for the rest of the week. In college it was pretty easy to have a social life, because everything was beside you. Now that we're all adults, people are either in a relationship or they're on the apps, I think.' Of the solitary nature of her work, she says, 'I think when you're farming, you're very tied to it. You can't get away, take time off. You can be very confined to it. I don't mind being alone.'

She doesn't use the apps herself, although she thinks they are the main way people have of meeting nowadays. From what friends tell her, they sound toxic. 'I don't think I would try them. It seems like they're only here for temporary things,' she says of men on dating apps. 'It's just to fill a void. That's how I feel about it. It's not genuine. Well, maybe the odd one. I wouldn't feel comfortable, I guess.' She does like Instagram though, 'just to have a conversation with someone'. From what she says, it feels like a safer space, somewhere she has also created a network with fellow young female farmers.

Other than that, if you want to meet someone, it's going out – not something she does a lot. 'If I go out, it's a big deal. You have to have your lift sorted and know what time you'll finish. It's a good half-hour run to anywhere.' You're relying on family and friends, or not drinking. 'A lot of people my sort of age would just drive to McDonald's and chat in the car. That would be the date.'

Until recently it was just Mark, on his school holidays, and his parents working on the farm. 'There was a good couple of years where the farm was expanding. With quotas going in 2015, and obviously we had bought the farm next door, there would have been a lot more of a workload. Up until 2019 we had a neighbour who used to milk for us, but apart from that it was just mom and dad, and me when I was at home.'

He recalls a teenage disco years ago where his friend gang was late because of him. 'I dunno, maybe an hour? And the bouncer lads were asking why were we late. They probably figured we had been drinking or something like

45

that. I said, "oh no, that was my fault, I had to put out sileage to the cows." All the lads had been waiting for me, and I was the one who delayed them. They could see we weren't drunk anyway.'

For years it was a heavy workload. 'Dad was saying when we were coming in the other day at five o'clock, "Gosh, even back five or six years ago, there was no coming in at five o'clock and being finished, like." Because there was stuff to be done.'

They have always worked hard, Mark says. 'To make life easier tomorrow. We're the kind of people that don't like to sit around doing nothing for too long. Sometimes you can feel guilty for taking time off, but I suppose it's important to know that it is important. There are other parts of your life that are a priority. If stuff needs to be done, I'll work until it's done. I'll work until eight or nine at night. But if you're finished your jobs at four o'clock, maybe you should take that early afternoon.'

When you love your work, as he does, it can be easy to keep going. In college, he used to play *Farming Simulator* on PlayStation. At home, he would play it after a full day's work. 'People used to be astonished, I'd just work all day on the farm, and I'd come in and play farming,' he laughs.

When he was at home full time, he found that he preferred to simply go back outside and keep working, rather than playing the simulation. 'I remember one evening, I was here by myself and I was playing it and I thought, I'd rather just be doing this in real life. So I went outside, it was about eight o'clock in the evening and I knew there was a bit of work I could do with the JCB, handy enough work to do, and I was like I'd rather just be doing this now than play-ing.' Farming isn't a clock-on-and-off thing, and neither is it a thing you fully retire from, he says. Mark talks about his grandfather, who, even when Mark's father fully took over, always remained involved in the work of the farm.

Now all the hard work is paying off. They have more people working with them and Mark hopes to take some time off next year, in the quieter months, for travel. His parents will encourage this. 'We're all working in the same direction for the farm … we have a very centrist mindset.'

It would be easy to become consumed by it, so it's important for him to remind himself that he is at a different stage in life to his father. He needs to allow room for other aspects to develop.

'Myself and my dad, we work a lot together. And obvi-ously we're at different parts of our life. If it was a Sunday, and he had nothing else to do, he'd be happy to go out and do a bit more work in the day on the farm, if he didn't want to rest or something. Maybe my mother's busy doing some-thing else, they're not going to go for a walk.' Mark has to remind himself that his father is married, that that part of his life is established. 'It's important to remember that maybe there's other aspects of my life that I need to focus on. There'll always be something to be done on a farm, there'll always be progress to be made, but sometimes you need to have priorities for other aspects of your life.'

He identifies three ways you might meet someone: ran-domly on a night out, through a club or hobby, or online. Mark is an active member of his local Macra (na Feirme, the countrywide voluntary rural youth organisation) and laughs when I put to him the idea that the organisation is Tinder for farmers. He clearly doesn't agree. 'It's just a social club for young adults, really. My club in Callan is a very strong club, very active. There's over a hundred members so it's really thriving. Which probably isn't the average in the country, they might be a bit smaller, mightn't be as active. When it gets going, it kind of catches fire, and people get more into it, you go to more events, and you get to know people better.'

Mark is a Macra baby, his own parents met in Macra. When he and his sister first attended their local club, they would arrive home and his parents would quiz them over their fellow members, offspring of their own generation.

'Dad and his brothers would have joined the local Macra when they moved here. There were a couple of branches trying to get them in. It was a way of getting to know everyone, and of having stuff to do. Back when they moved up, in the eighties, sure there wasn't much to do.'

On nights out Mark and his friends would typically go into Kilkenny. Transport is 'a bit of a challenge', he says. 'But sure, you might either drive in and just leave the car there and pick it up tomorrow, or get someone to drop you in, and it's usually an expensive taxi ride out. Because we're farming, often you have to be up at six o'clock the following morning. You just accept that and think, I'll just lose out on the sleep, otherwise I'll never get to go out.'

During the spring months, he is probably working a hundred hours a week, maybe more – 'in the peak of it, it's work, eat and sleep.' Mark rolls out of bed at six and goes straight to work, in for breakfast a few hours later. At lunchtime, everyone working on the farm congregates in the kitchen to make rolls and sandwiches for themselves.

He's not hugely positive about clubs of the Macra – or night – variety as places to meet someone. 'You're generally going to know the people there, and unless someone new comes in it's unlikely that there's anything going to happen there,' he says of the former. 'And then, try and meet someone on a night out: it depends, if you're in a pub maybe, but if you're in a club ...' He shrugs. 'It's kind of hard to meet someone you're going to develop a relationship with, I feel, anyway.'

As for the apps? 'Ah sure they're touch and go really,' he says, leaning back in his chair, crossing his arms and grinning. 'And then you get sick of it.' He would set the radius narrow enough to begin with, 'but then you just run out of people.'

'I know in the past, anytime I've used an app you'll set the range really small, and then you have to keep upping it every now and again. If you go into a town or a city you could set it at a real small distance and there's loads of people around. But in a rural scene, you have to set it quite wide.'

'You do come across people you know on the apps alright, but I don't think there's too much awkwardness with it because it's a common occurrence nowadays, everyone is using them. It can be quite difficult to meet people in person.' Mark has been in two relationships: he met one of his girlfriends through events in college, the other locally.

Nearly everyone is on the dating apps, he says, adding that he is not suited to the kind of communication they require. 'I'm terrible at texting people. I can talk away to people grand, but when it comes to generating conversation through text, I'm not good at it. Even my family or my friends will say that. Most of my friends I don't text on a regular basis at all. I've friends who I might text twice a year, but you're still close friends when you meet up. So that's kind of a big barrier for me.'

How important is it to him to meet someone who is also in farming, who already shares the lifestyle he so loves? 'You'd really limit your options then,' he replies. 'Obviously agriculture is predominantly men. It's great, there is a lot more women getting involved in it,' but not to the extent where he could decide to only date farmers. Actually, it might get trickier, he points out, 'if I was to meet someone who was also farming. Both of my previous girlfriends were not from farming backgrounds. Taking over the farm here as well, I'm kind of tied. It would probably get a little bit more complicated if you were to meet someone who is in a similar situation, who isn't up the road but a good few kilometres away, and they're also into the farming, and they're going to inherit their farm. It's a little bit ahead of me,' he laughs bashfully, 'but that can be challenging alright. It depends on the individuals.'

It's an assumption many of the people I talk to make, that if they meet someone that person is unlikely to live near them. It's made more complicated for those in farming, a profession that makes one immovable.

'It is something that always comes to mind,' Sophie says of this conundrum, 'because they will probably be a farmer. I won't know how to engage with someone who doesn't really understand. I think that ... I guess it would depend on the income of the other farmer, maybe.'

So it would come down to who had the best farm? Others I speak to suggest that traditionally, social and family expectations would have been for the woman to move farm, without question. 'Yeah, unfortunately.' I don't get the sense Sophie will make any move that doesn't suit her.

There's another way in which Mark and Sophie are similar, in fact they 'know of' each other because of it. Both Mark and Sophie are agri-influencers – a rather lovely offshoot of the typical influencer stock-in-trade that deals in shopping hauls and make-up videos. Instead, from agri-influencers you are more likely to see barns being hosed down, silage pits, tractors pushing out on a rainy day; #gifted content will be feeding paraphernalia or outdoor weather gear. Sophie has been an agri-influencer for about four years. She has that funny combination you often see in influencers, talking confidently to thousands online (Sophie has almost 20,000 followers), but in person quiet and reserved, quite shy. While her content may differ from other influencers – and agri-influencing seems like a more wholesome corner of the web than most – she is, like most women online, subjected to weird comments on her Instagram, a lot of them sexualised, she says.

For Mark, it's something he first got involved in because he noticed people beginning to care more about where their food was coming from, but he felt there was a lot of misinformation online. 'Years ago in Ireland most people would be only one or two generations away from someone who was farming. Or they might have a relative who was farming. Whereas nowadays a large percentage of the

51

population has no connection whatsoever. People have no idea where their food comes from or how it's produced.'

He had originally planned to do YouTube videos, something he now puts a lot of time and work into filming and editing, but his sister suggested he try Instagram first to build up a following – it's an easier platform to get started on. 'I'm doing the Instagram now for a couple of years, three years maybe this summer, and also doing the YouTube there just over a year as well.'

He's very proud of their farm – 'we have a very good farm here' – and likes showcasing how they are doing. There's a community of farmers online, YouTubers and Instagrammers learning from each other, he explains, sort of online discussion groups. And people loved it, he says with a grin. People who have nothing to do with farming really enjoy the content, his everyday business.

For Sophie, Instagram has given her a rather satisfying ability to push back at existing stereotypes about what makes a farmer. Simply by putting herself and her work online, she undermines existing notions of what a farmer looks like – that is, not male.

She thinks that women are often not taken seriously in farming matters. 'It's a matter of proving yourself. In my case, because I'm a young girl just out of college.' Many of the workspaces she enters are male – the mart, for example. 'It's intimidating. You do feel like you're the only woman in the room. Being taken seriously is something that I would think about when I'm going in. I guess I just get on with it.'

I ask if there are any other challenges facing women in farming. 'I think we have to look a certain way. Like, I would want to wear make-up when I am farming. Some people would say, "Is she a real famer?"'

Aisling Molloy is a Future Beef Programme adviser with Teagasc, based in Mallow, County Cork. Her master's thesis looked at the empowerment of farm women, and some of the issues challenging that. Aisling herself grew up on a farm, one she hopes to eventually inherit. Sophie and Aisling's experiences aren't always typical, often a male will still inherit even if the daughter of the family shows more of an interest in the farm. 'In Ireland, there's huge pride associated with the family farm because we're so attached to land. It's in our blood. That is a huge barrier on the female side,' Aisling explains of the importance placed on the family name remaining on the farm, and how this can mean women will often not inherit the family farm even though they are the ones most invested in it.

In her work for her master's, Aisling spoke to 233 farm women in County Wexford, and identified several impediments to women's engagement in farming. Traditionally, a lot of the work women did on farms was unpaid and somewhat invisible. Women themselves, both those of previous generations and those Aisling spoke to several years ago, often discounted the importance of their work on the farm, tasks that might include 'calf-rearing, looking after the young stock, feeding hens, growing veg and trying to run a full family home as well'.

In more recent times, the amount of administration involved in running a farm has increased massively. When Aisling asked the women about their role on the farm, 'they would have said "oh I don't play a role"', when in fact they were looking after immense amounts of paperwork, dealing with Department of Agriculture schemes, suppliers, involved in management decisions, feeding, farm labour and ordering supplies.

One major issue for women in farming is visibility, Aisling explains. If you can't see it, you can't be it. 'There's a tendency for some people in the industry to assume that all farmers are male. So if they're speaking about it, they'll say, "he does this, he'll do that". It's very patronising, as a woman, to hear that.' Whether true or not, there was a real sense amongst the women she spoke to that they were not taken as seriously as men, and that they were not welcome in agricultural groups such as discussion forums.

For now, Sophie helps her parents run the farm. They all live in a house on the land. Her grandparents' house, where her father grew up, is down the lane. Even though not everyone earns their living from the farm, it is a communal affair. 'I feel like everyone's involved, together. You'd all sit round the table and discuss aspects of the farm.'

The farm has been in her family since the 1960s, her grandfather's time. Both her parents are in their fifties and working full-time jobs off farm, which they now wish to focus on solely. Sophie has been working a second job, as well as milking on another farm. She's not sure when she takes over the farm herself whether she will keep up this level of work. Farming full time might not allow her to get a mortgage, so she thinks it's quite likely she will need to have two jobs.

What will the change actually mean for her? 'I will be in charge of the money, and what happens, basically. Dad says he'll definitely help but that will be physical help.'

She's not really nervous, she muses in her soft tones, carefully pulling back an electric wire between fields for me to walk around. Her youth and subsequent lack of responsibilities actually take the pressure off and allow room for error. 'If I did it when I was thirty, I'd probably have my own accommodation and financial ties. There's not as much pressure at the moment. Even though I am young, it's a good time to make mistakes. I don't have a house or anything like that, it's a good time to learn. It's a lot of responsibility, because you have to keep things right, meet all the targets and stuff. I think if I stress about it, it'll just make it worse.'

Giving up is always an option, but not an appealing one, and not one I get the impression she has considered. The running of a family farm isn't simply a job you walk away from in favour of another if things don't work out. Sophie is a link in a chain of inheritance. And there is the perception element of it. How it would look.

'I think if everything went wrong, you could definitely sell it, and it's a big asset to have. Not that I'd take this into account, but I do think that if you sell the farm, it's deemed a failure by other farmers.' In fact, it's striking that for those I speak to who are taking over their family farms, now or in the future, there's a sort of peacefulness to the foregone nature of it. There's something lovely about being happy enough with the life you were brought up in to actively want to continue that into adulthood.

On a second visit, I speak to Steph, Sophie's mother. We're in the kitchen when she comes bustling in, surrounded by several dogs who all flock to her. She's home from a day's work in a local business. Now fifty-four, she came to the farm when she was twenty-three – Sophie's age – moving from Derby, England because of her relationship with her now husband, and first living with her in-laws-to-be. We sit in her kitchen in the house she and her husband built after they got married and when Steph was pregnant with Sophie's older brother. It lies just up the lane from her husband's family home. She is a warm, chatty, vibrant person, clearly the centre of this home. When I put it to her how Aisling's research shows that much of the farm work undertaken by women is invisible and undervalued, I see a gleam in her eye, and it feels as if I have hit a nerve. As well as crucial farm work – looking after milking, calving, ordering supplies, feeding everyone – Steph worked a number of part-time jobs at night or during school hours to avoid the need for childcare, raised two children and ran a home. How does she feel about Sophie taking over the farm? 'There's a completely different outlook on everything now. She's got enough sense and feistiness in her to know you don't have to go through such hardship. I think everything then had to be hardship. When you could get a tractor in to bring out dung, do it in the *barra* [wheelbarrow].

'I think with the young ones these days, there's so much thought goes into it, and the organisation end of things, to get the best result that you can with sort of a bit of ease from it. It doesn't have to be blood, sweat and tears to get the finished result that you need. I think it's probably a different train of thought.'

There's the fact that they've all had to take the Green Cert, a qualification that allows for certain grants, or gone to college. These things instil a confidence that previous generations maybe didn't have.

Steph describes the pace of her life. 'You were kind of juggling everything. I would work [off the farm] from ten till two Monday to Friday, do everything that was needed with the suckler cows before I went, especially in calving time, get two kids out to school, off down to work. You'd come home at two, fling some kind of dinner in [the oven], but before that you would have checked to see was anything happening. If there was anything dangling out of the backside of a cow I would run for Sean next door, and me and him would try and calve this cow that we had no idea what stage she was at, because you hadn't seen her for the last four hours.'

We talk about how proud of her daughter she is and Steph, who is upbeat and funny and full of laughter, unexpectedly wells up with pride in her impressive daughter. 'I hope Sophie's generation of farmers is well enough travelled and educated to have an open mind, and will now run their farms as businesses, rather than something they were saddled with all of their adult life, missing opportunities, getting that fun and enjoyment in your work rather than turning it into a form of torture.'

4

A Bit of a Change

Erica grew up on a 65-acre farm in north county Cork. During her childhood years it was a mixed farm with cows, pigs, sheep, tillage and beekeeping. The pigs were phased out early, then the sheep, and a dairy herd was built up with pedigree Friesian cattle. In time the necessity of a large investment in building new dairy equipment became clear, but the cost was too high, so Erica's father decided to sell the dairy herd and rear calves for beef. Even as a child, Erica was very involved in the running of the farm. She was originally born a boy into a family of three, the middle child, with an older sister and a younger brother. It would be years before she came out as a transgender woman.

Of her childhood she says, 'I always worked: home from school, out working till night. It was hard work at the time, but you're born into it and you didn't kind of question it.'

As adulthood approached, she never considered leaving the farm. 'At times I would have liked to, but I thought I was responsible, that … 'twas my duty to keep the show on the road, keep things going. I'd probably love to have gone into engineering, I could make or do anything. Once I could figure out how a thing worked, I could tear it apart and fix it.'

Growing up, she didn't have much of a social life. There wasn't much to do, and she was, 'a bit shy myself. One night I was to go to a Macra event. I got an invitation from the local branch. There was something that night something needed to be done on the farm, so I couldn't go to it. Sure, I never bothered again.' The nature of the work on the farm, and the way the farm was run, meant she was 'very tied down'.

Erica is sixty-seven now. She inherited the farm several years ago, when her father, a few months short of ninety, passed away. Until his death, the farm was run by him. 'In a lot of ways, he was a very good person. He'd no understanding of other people, that was the trouble. Life wasn't easy with him.'

Both her parents came from farming backgrounds, moving to this farm to raise their own family. Erica was close to her mother, who died years before she inherited the farm. 'She was a great worker, a very good cook.' They got on most of the time, she says, adding with a laugh: 'we'd always have an argument at some point. She loved gardening … great cook … knitting, embroidery.'

She was also interested in music, something they shared. When Erica eventually got her own car, they would take off in it together, going to concerts. 'I went on my own as well at times.' The car meant an improvement in terms of her independence, but there was still a sense of being monitored by the patriarch of the farm.

'You were expected to be back at a certain time. Even if I came up to Cork to get a part for a machine or something, if the first place you went to hadn't got it, you might go to two or three places, it was difficult to get stuff because some of the machinery was old, getting a bit obsolete – when you got back, you'd be asked what kept you.'

'You'd be out shopping, out for a Sunday drive, doing anything, you could be eaten raw.' She laughs as she recalls an incident: 'One year we went up to Cork Summer Show, myself and the mother, he didn't go. He was a year talking about the work he did the day we went to the show. There was more work done that day … it was the busiest day of the year.' It didn't feel like there were many options beyond the farm as Erica became an adult. It wasn't until her forties that she first worked off the farm, part-time with a rural development scheme. Getting out was 'a great release'.

She took part in a personal development course run by Avondhu Blackwater Partnership, which was a 'ferocious help all together' in terms of confidence. 'It actually probably made me. At home I was only looked at as being the spare vice grips. Repair and repair. Down there it was the first time that I saw that I'd way more ability.' She took part in university-level tests, 'things that I should have been bogged down with, but I wasn't. That was a great booster for me.' She was told that instead of farming she should be attending UCC's adult education courses.

Erica describes going back home afterwards. 'I thought I'd go away and tidy up the farm, make changes that made it a lower work rate, but sure I just could do nothing with the father. Nothing could be changed. Slog away so.'

She and her father were engaged in a farm partnership, but it wasn't in truth an equal arrangement. 'He was chief executive and ruler,' she chuckles. There was a resistance to change, new machinery, replacing anything that had broken. To any new ways of doing things. 'Everything had to be done the hardest way. The shovel and the pike and the pickaxe. The hardest way it could be done.'

Was she an employee of the farm until her father passed away? 'General dogsbody,' Erica grins. She wasn't paid a wage, but rather could draw from the farm's account for day-to-day living expenses. Occasionally, in her younger years, she would go to dances, socials run by the church. 'Other places as well. Creed or no creed. Ordinary ballrooms. Lovely music, dancing and that as well. I'd go there and sometimes there were some girls now I'd kind of like. Never got down to trying to make a relationship but there's no doubt the lack of a decent income on the farm was one big barrier at times. You couldn't see the farm sustaining another family coming up. That's probably one of my faults as well. I think things through a lot. Analyse everything. I think a good bit before I do things. What are the consequences? There's always consequences of everything.'

It took decades before Erica realised that she was transgender. 'When I was growing up, I didn't even know what a transgender was. I used to hear [the phrase] LGBT, but I didn't know what the "T" stood for, and I was one of them. I knew what the others were, but I didn't know what that was.'

One Friday night, when she was in her fifties, she was watching *The Late Late Show*. 'This lady came on, and she had been born a man, and changed. She told her story, and it just rang true, it ticked my boxes. That was what I was.'

She had always known there was something she didn't quite understand about herself, and describes how, as a small child aged five or six, she had hated getting her hair cut short.

'I didn't know there was such a thing as you could be born what I call a bit of a mix-up. Be born your body in one zone, your mind in another zone. I didn't know what anything about transgender was, I didn't even realise that was a possibility. I was always drawn more to female-type clothes. Bit by bit it got more feminine, then it was quite feminine in the end.'

She describes the burden on her mental health over the years. 'I didn't care whether I lived or died for a long time.' She became unwell, suspected she had bowel cancer, but didn't bother going to get checked out. Eventually she decided to find out how long she had left so that she could get her affairs in order. 'I didn't care if it took me.' As it turned out, she did not have cancer.

Seeing her story reflected back at her from the *Late Late* that night brought a massive sense of relief. 'There was a big change, because I knew what I was then. I didn't actually realise that you could be born partly male and partly female. Whatever way you want to put it, 'tis the same either direction. When she said her feelings and the story, the whole thing matched to me. And I said that's what I was.'

She explains how, several years before she came out, she 'went looking' on the internet, searching in Google:

How do you know you're trans? 'One advice was to open an email account in your new name, subscribe to a few things and get emails back. Another thing was choosing colours, looking at colours. Everything came up that I was a female. And paint your nails. See does it feel right. My answer was definitely yes.'

Still though, she was unable to come out, that would not happen until after her father passed away. 'You just said you'd kind of live with it. I could tell nobody. That was very difficult. I just couldn't pick out the purpose of life.'

She notes two things that comforted her. 'There was one time now, we had a collie dog, Lassie, she'd be one of the most beautiful people if she was a person. She could just read you like a book. If you were down, she'd shower love and affection.'

The other thing was listening to music. 'I love classical music. I'd go down in the room and lie on the carpet in the darkness and turn on the symphony or something and just lose myself in it. You'd get lost in it.'

'Often, I'd just go down to the room and stay there. Get stuck into the internet or something. I was involved in another few things then, in investment clubs. You'd invest fifty euros a month in buying shares and selling them. We'd meet up once a month or so.' With shares from the investment club Erica was eventually able to buy herself a tractor.

Her father died suddenly. Erica found him in his bed. 'That was a bit of a shock. But he never wanted to go in hospital, he always said he'd love to die in the yard with the boots on. He got a more comfortable way.' For the last year or two of his life he was mostly around the house, but before that, even in his eighties, he would be doing a little bit all the time. 'He was a fierce worker. Manual hardship jobs, the harder the better.'

One day two years later, in 2019, in Cork city where she had gone to get her new glasses, Erica, now in her sixties, had a moment that changed her life.

'I came out of the shop. I went over to Debenhams. I wanted some mascara. I was walking past the Lancôme counter, this girl came over to me and said, "Can I help you?" I said I was interested in some mascara, and she said no problem. She says there's a lot of men experimenting in make-up now. She was so kind and nice, that it came out of me. That I was transgender. First person to say it to in the world.'

She refers to Nelson Mandela talking about the freedom he felt after leaving prison. 'I was like Mandela,' Erica beams. 'It just came out. She was so kind and supportive. I just couldn't stop it. There's a saying, women always get their way. Erica got her way that day.'

Two years earlier, in 2017, she had got a tiny tattoo on her shoulder – unbeknownst to anyone else – of the name 'Erica' in Japanese hiragana. 'Just a small little thing. I was going to be Erica myself even though I couldn't tell anybody at the time,' Now though, there was no stopping her. 'Everyone was told then. As they say the jail gate was open, and I felt free.'

She called one neighbour, another farmer. 'I told him on the phone. I said, "Jim have you heard the latest scandal about me?" He said, "what?" And I told him. I told him that I'm transgender and that I'm coming out. He said, "I was suspecting something, and when you say it now, the more I think of it, that's where the pink runners are coming from.'"

Like all her neighbours and her community, he was fully supportive. Later, he told Erica, 'you were the talk of the place for a week and then it was forgotten about.' Did the uniformly positive reaction of her neighbours surprise her? 'I was definitely surprised at some of them. I expected some of them would be okay, because they respected me so much, no matter what I did. More of them I was surprised. Once I came out, even if there were a few nasty comments, it wouldn't change anything.'

Telling another neighbour, the woman replied, 'I was admiring your nails. And my daughters were remarking something went wrong before you were born, you should have been a girl.' Erica lifts a hand to show me her bright red polish. Someone said to her once: what are you doing painting your nails, just on the farm with cows? 'It isn't for other people at all, I'm doing it for me. When I've my nails done, one of the first things I do in the morning is look at them, and it feels right. And then looking down at a skirt, it's just totally correct.'

She describes her comfort in farming spaces, traditionally areas that are male dominated. "Twasn't long out down at Macroom mart, and I wore a skirt that day now. A few people I know now, they just took no notice.' Shortly afterwards she attended a large IFA meeting, which drew a big crowd. Afterwards, Erica went for a drink in the bar.

'There were two other fells from Macroom, I don't know who they were. Chatting away about different things, the meeting, cattle and things, and one of them said to me what part of the country do you come from missus,' she recalls with delight. 'The fear was a lot worse than the reality of it. That's what I think about life: the fear of a lot of things is worse than going ahead and doing it, no matter what it is.'

Inheriting the farm at the age of sixty-three has challenges. 'I'm free to do things now, but the trouble is my health isn't as good now. Trouble with my knees at the moment now. So it's hard to do work. So I don't know, we'll have to see how things work out. Tipping away at the farm now anyway.'

She talks about the possibility of renting or selling it, if running things became too much. But then what? 'The place I was born and reared. 'Tis home. Would any place ever become home again? I don't know. Where you go then is another thing. If I need somebody at three o'clock in the morning, it's a case of which one of the neighbours will I ring. And they'd be there.'

Her conversation is peppered with mention of neighbours who stepped in to look after the farm at times she was unwell, and invitations of dinner issued. She has a skill that has meant she has helped many in her community: Erica practises dowsing. Also referred to as divining, it is the practice of using rods or sticks to look for objects hidden underground, things both visible and not, water, minerals and energy. Erica and her father visited a faith healer years ago, when her father was unwell, and the man told her then that she could do what he did.

'He showed me how to do it. I found out I could do certain things with people, horses and dogs, never cattle. Couldn't do any healing with them or find out anything about them. He showed us how to do it with two bits of coat hangers in an L-shape. Bad energy lines, underground water lines, magnetic pollution, stray electric fields can mean ill health in humans and animals.

Now her services are regularly sought. She has gone as far as Turkey with her dowsing, although the work can be draining so it is not something she does regularly. But listening to her, you get the sense that this is something that has further knitted her into her community and is a source of pride for her.

'I start at your front door with my wires, have my two wires in my hands, if I come over a bad energy line, the wires cross.' In one case she attended an eight-day-old baby who was having difficulty hearing. After Erica worked on her, the child was cured. It's work that brings her a great deal of satisfaction and respect. 'There'd be some people who might laugh at the idea but sure, *lave* them,' she says in her gentle lilt. 'A lot of my life is disappointing. What I achieved. What I wanted to achieve but couldn't. But when people tell you what you did for them, 'tis nice actually.'

After coming out, it felt as if 'a fierce weight' had lifted. 'I'm myself now. Even other people have said it to me since I came out.' There was the rector in her Church of Ireland parish. 'After I telling him, he said you're changed completely, you can see it in your face. You're so content and happy looking now compared to before.'

She recalls how, after a funeral, she talked to a retired Catholic parish priest she is friendly with. 'I told him that I was born a bit mixed up. I said to him, "I'm after making a bit of a change." He looked down and he said, "I see that." I said, "I was born a bit of a mix up." He said, "You weren't born a mix up at all. Children are born in all kinds of different ways, and the Lord loves them all." It felt really good actually. He said a prayer for me, gave me a blessing and everything.'

For the first time in her life, Erica began to like her reflection when she looked in the mirror. 'I always used to hate myself in photographs. I remember now one time in Cork, I had a bit of make-up on, and I got another bit done. A lovely girl down in Brown Thomas this time now. Came home then and looked in the mirror. It was the first time I liked myself in my life. Another time you could be at a wedding, you would have a suit, done up, people would be telling you, "You're very dapper today." I couldn't see it at all. I always looked totally wrong. It was the first time I thought I looked right.' She is proud of herself. 'I don't think I've anything to be ashamed of,' she reflects.

Her local GP has been supportive, as has the Cork Gender Support Group. She is moving slowly through the process of transitioning. 'I'll do one step at a time. I'll go a lot of the way anyway.' She's not sure what to expect once she begins hormones, has been told that that will change things quite a lot. 'Your feelings will be all changed. You'll be totally different. So I don't know what to expect there, I've no idea.' It means that a relationship isn't really in her thoughts for now.

'At the moment, I'm on the road I am now. I'm happier now. Go for your beliefs. Just go for it, if you have a dream in life.'

5

Tinder for Farmers and Someone to Talk To

Several years ago, in an interview shortly after taking on the role, the newly elected president of Macra na Feirme, James Healy, told C103's *Cork Today* that the organisation he now led was the 'unofficial dating agency of rural Ireland. Who needs Tinder when you can join Macra?'

Macra is *absolutely* better than Tinder, Kerry man John Martin Carroll tells me firmly. John lives in Causeway and works for Macra as its Student Agriculture Development Officer. He has also run a number of Macra dating events and charity fundraisers. And when we speak, he is the reigning Mr Personality, one of the big annual Macra events. Others include Queen of the Land, Miss Blue Jeans and Miss Macra.

Now thirty-five years old, John joined Macra in 2016. There is a sense it came into his life when he was feeling a little lost. He had had a particularly tough couple of years previously, losing both of his parents to cancer and having himself undergone an operation years earlier to remove a cancerous tumour in his lung.

'Two friends came into the yard, and they said, "Will you join Macra?" I said, "That's for farmers." But I signed up, and it was the best thing that ever happened me. It changed my life completely. You're having fun, you're meeting like-minded people, there's a certain amount of them farmers.' He compares Mr Personality to the Rose of Tralee.

'There's three judges and a host. You go up, you talk, you say what you've done with Macra, and you can do a party piece if you want to. The first year I didn't get through, but the second year I did qualify. My party piece was a little poem.'

'I'll explain,' he says, going back to the dating apps and why Macra is better. 'Because I'm just after deleting Tinder for the 500th time. I'm happy with the way I look, but what I've learnt is, I feel like Tinder's like a mart. And I don't like that. You see a photo of me, I could fill out a profile, but I'm totally different if you meet me in person. I feel it brings down confidence and everything. It has for me anyway.' He has been on and off Tinder for years but has met far more people through Macra.

'With Macra, you can go in and say what club you're with, what activities you like, because everyone is … we're from the same kind of background. The *amount* of people I've met who have the same interests as me. It makes it a lot easier to have a conversation, or to get to know some-one, compared to Tinder.'

John is not alone in finding the manner of communication on Tinder difficult. He describes feeling a pressure to be entertaining in online messages. 'I'm not a texter. If you say *Hi, how are you?* that's not good enough. You have to do something creative. And then I feel like I'm in the middle of a circus, jumping through hoops.' He feels there is a falsity to whatever intimacy or impressions online exchanges establish. 'I land, and then they roll their eyes because I'm not what they want.'

John finds it hard to be himself on dates made through Tinder, whereas the atmosphere of a Macra event is 'very relaxed'. There's also the fact that the distances involved with people he might meet through online dating can be problematic. John likes his established community, something Macra only builds on. He met a woman online who was a farmer, but it became an issue that they lived so far apart. 'What's the middle ground? What will I do? I've family here, friends here, the community, activities.'

Far easier to try to meet someone at Macra dinner dances. 'It's like a wedding without the bride and the groom. Compared to a nightclub which, my dear god, looking back is insanity,' he sighs. He finds it almost impossible to approach women at a nightclub. 'I do like going out in Killarney but it's so hard to meet someone out in a pub or a nightclub.'

Bouncers don't have much work to do at Macra events, it seems. 'I've had events where I was dancing on the stage and the bouncer was standing beside me. There's no fighting, there's music, there's people that will just come up and say "Hi, how are you, where are you from?" The first time I had that at a Macra event, I was like, what's their fucking problem?' he laughs.

71

John goes on to describe what he is looking for in a partner. 'I want someone, but I don't want ... forget looks, it's interests, hobbies, a connection. I want someone who will have the same sense of humour, gets who I am, and who's just happy to be, I suppose, together.'

In a way, what he's describing is Macra as a kind of IRL niche dating app, a forum that puts you in the way of people who have similar interests, priorities, way of life.

Daniel got involved in Macra through friends when he was around seventeen, about ten years ago. He's now the PR officer of the Muskerry Macra branch. He talks about it in similar terms to John, as a means of connecting with like-minded people. 'You meet people who are in the same kind of world as you, with the same interests.'

Since he joined his branch, which has a membership of approximately 150, thirteen long-term relationships have formed, out of which have been nine marriages, two engagements and, he thinks, seven babies. 'It doesn't just harvest relationships, it harvests long-term relationships' he adds.

Daniel is from County Cork. He doesn't work in farming. 'When you're in a place like where I'm from, the only things that are happening are Macra things. Once you finish youth clubs when you're like fifteen, *latest*, after that it's either Macra or the pub.'

He assumes that I've probably heard Macra is all about the pub. Actually, the overriding – and erroneous – impression of Macra I have come across is that it is for older people, rather than the membership of 17–35-year-olds it actually boasts. In fact, it seems a remarkably vibrant organisation, centred around the events run for members: everything from walks to water sports to black-tie balls to public-speaking competitions. It acts as a sort of fulcrum, pulling the local community together.

'The first event I really remember was a soapbox race that ran over at the hill near my house. Teams from all over the country made soapboxes and raced them down the hill.' During lockdown, Daniel ran online speed-dating events for Macra members all over the country. 'Everyone got five dates, they were all ten or fifteen minutes long. There's a lot of creativity goes into these events.' The more exercised the members running a local Macra are, the more popular a club seems to be.

If you're working on an isolated farm, Macra offers you a way to meet people beyond the local pub, Daniel says. 'And to do things outside of your comfort zone, for anyone up to the age of thirty-five. There's a lot of people who, if they don't know anything about Macra, just think it's a drinking thing. Nearly everybody thinks it's a load of men, yet 45 per cent of the membership is female. There are 10,000 members nationwide.'

Before his girlfriend met him, she probably would have thought Macra was a load of farmers, he says. 'A load of farmers, doing farmery things in fields at the weekend, talking about cows, and then going to the pub. But there's so much more to it. It's an organisation for people in the countryside. Farming is in the title, there's no denying it, but the 21st-century version of Macra is a social outlet that helps young people get to meet new people and try new things.'

GAA is a huge outlet, but if you're not interested in sport 'you're kind of snookered', Daniel adds. 'That's where Macra would come in, bring you out of your comfort zone and get you meeting new people. Not everyone's interested in sports, and that's where oftentimes country towns get a bit snookered.'

Fintan had always wanted to join Macra, finally getting around to attending the Trim branch in early 2020. Not ideal timing to join an organisation the point of which is to make in-person connections within your community. He liked it from the outset. 'I thought it was grand. Thought it was fine and dandy: this is great. Went to the first meeting, thought I'll get used to this, and then all of a sudden, bang, the whole country just went on its knees like.' We're sitting over hot drinks outside a café near Fintan's family home. It's a January evening and cold, the light dying as we talk. At twenty-one years old, he is a large, squarely built man, a slightly incongruous match for the heavily decorated hot chocolate laden with frilly rings of cream that has arrived at our table and over which he hunches.

Macra had appealed to Fintan because he felt he would find 'people who'd have the same interests. I always thought it was for people that were farmers, but sure I'm in Trim Macra, half of them are not farmers'.

Fintan explains that he sometimes finds it hard to talk to people. Growing up, he didn't have friends, something he puts down to being autistic and having been diagnosed with ADHD as a child. 'Being painted with the brush that you're weird, and you're different, it is hard going through school. A lot of the lads that I was in school with thought well, you're fucking different.'

He didn't grow up on a farm, but that life always held an attraction. From childhood he always wanted to own a tractor. Fintan grew up on a housing estate in Trim where he still lives but spent time on his uncle's farm as a child, and it made an impression. His father, who he's close to, grew up in Tipperary and drove tractors for the neighbouring families. Now Fintan owns two tractors and works part-time as a farm labourer. 'I like driving, that's the be-all and end-all of it. I like driving,' he says firmly. He also regularly does charity tractors meets and road runs.

Lockdown meant it was many months before he got to go to another Macra evening after that first event. This time it was a dating event held in a hotel and based on a mart, in which fellow members bid on each other rather than live-stock. 'It's like a cattle mart but it's for males and females. So you bid for them, the men and women get sold off.' Fintan actually applied to be one of the men for sale. 'But I didn't get it. They had enough people by the time I applied for it, so I didn't get a place.'

There was an auctioneer from a cattle mart running the bidding and everyone at the event was given Macra money. Ten euro was a hundred in Macra money.

'I knew two people going in, and I walked away knowing about twenty,' Fintan says. 'That's one thing about Macra, you will find people who have the same interests. It was great craic. I loved it. I didn't leave it until one in the morning.'

Almost immediately, things got underway and he began bidding, he remembers with a smile. 'I was impatient, I should have waited. I was itching at the bit.' Unfortunately, he and the woman he bid on only exchanged a brief 'hello' and then didn't speak for the rest of the night. Instead, he hit it off with a woman at his table. 'The girl that I should have bought, we haven't stopped talking since.' He went to buy her when her turn came up, but wasn't allowed, having already had a successful bid. 'They won't let you buy two, you see.'

He knows a lot of couples who met through Macra. 'I just want to get on with it,' he says, echoing John's sentiment. 'I want something else bar work. I've a lovely family, but I need something that is not my family. Who I can go and talk to, and love. Someone to spend money on. Someone to talk to.'

6

The Home Place

There are several things that can make having a relationship tricky for a farmer. Firstly, there is the inheritance timeline. The senior farmer is unlikely to retire before some time in their sixties. Even then, they will probably keep up a certain level of involvement in the farm. In many cases, a farm will only provide enough for one income, or the support of one family.

Where does this leave the child-then-adult who is to inherit? They will eventually take on the responsibility, but by the time their parent is ready to cede primary running of the farm the inheritor will be well into adulthood. They will have reached a time when they will have had to make inroads into setting up a sustainable life for themselves and possibly be supporting a family. This might mean work entirely off farm, or a split working life between the farm and work elsewhere. Or they may have stayed on the farm, eked out a life there, but not necessarily be in a position to support a family.

One farmer I spoke to who didn't inherit the farm until their sixties described worrying about how they would support a family, as the farm was barely providing for the people living there. It made them hesitant in beginning relationships.

There is this, and then there are the long days involved in this kind of work, and the fact that many farmers are unlikely to have on-site support who can cover evenings off, step in at emergencies (animals escaping though broken fences or getting ill), or run things if the owner decides to take a holiday. It's not a lifestyle that is conducive to an active dating life.

From when he was little, Edward loved the lifestyle of the place where he grew up. The family farm which he will inherit is just outside Gorey, an eighty-acre sheep farm fragmented into three parts. Now thirty-two years old, and the eldest in his family, from the age of three Edward was out on the farm as much as he could be. 'Mammy couldn't keep me in, I was going around on my toy tractor,' he laughs.

'We're very much a sheep farm, we love working with sheep at home.' Edward has a very gentle way about him. 'I think anyone who grows up being hands-on with livestock, you have a different set of emotions towards looking after something.'

'I'd have no problem staying up all night with a sick animal. You do your utmost for it, even when at times you probably know you're going down a losing track. I think that empathy just resonates very much with people who come from a rural or farming background.'

It also informs your dealings with people, he says. In his last job, Edward had a team of forty people reporting to him.

'For myself, I have greater empathy towards people when they've been dealing with issues. I could listen to people more openly, and sort of understand where they were coming from, their worries or issues.'

Edward is the eldest of six, with one brother and four sisters. 'My great-grandmother would have been the main farmer back in the day. Daddy grew up with her teaching him a lot of the stuff on the farm. It's been handed down for several generations, and it's down to me now.' He will be the sixth generation of his family to run this farm.

Although his siblings have all developed careers of their own, it wasn't a given that he would be the one to take over eventually. 'Everyone had a keen interest in the farm. Daddy and Mammy always brought whoever was interested into that life,' he says of his parents, who met at a showband night.

He describes the manner in which his parents navigated the potentially fraught issue of which child inherits the farm while maintaining clarity around succession.

'It really comes down to the parents being open when you're a child and while growing up. It wasn't a conversation that came up every month, it was just from time to time, that ultimately the farm would go to one of us. It's important that the parents are not afraid to say that, so that everyone grows up with an awareness of the family situation.'

The size of the farm wouldn't lend it to being broken up into smaller sizes, he points out. It's not just the practicalities of how breaking up a property would undermine the farm that matter. Not splitting the farm between all the siblings is a matter of respect towards his parents, and the effort they have put in over their working lifetime. 'How the parents would like to see it going in the next generation' is important to Edward.

'Our farm isn't a big farm. There's six of us, if we were to divide that farm evenly, it would all break down to small bits of land. There might be six smaller-scale farms, but the fabric of the farm that the parents have built up wouldn't be the same.' For him, it's about respecting their wishes. He is conscious that they have put in a lifetime of work. 'They want to see you maintain that and bring it on to another level. I suppose for any parents there is fear – and I'd say it's very relatable to anyone whose family has a business – that one generation will spend a lot building it up, and the next … will they always do the same? Or will all their hard work just go away in one generation?'

He repeats something his father says on the matter. 'Daddy always quotes at home, there comes a gatherer or there comes a scatterer. One generation could give everything to build it up, and then the next generation will just come along and flutter it away with no care for what the previous generation has done.'

Their farm would not support two full-time incomes. Edward's 58-year-old father is very active on the farm. This means that, for now, the son works elsewhere for his living: a nine-to-five Monday-to-Friday position as an engineer in a large company in Wexford. Edward fits his farming work around the day job.

'Daddy works full time on the farm, I work full time off the farm, but I'm also on the farm in the evenings and at the weekend.' He lives in what was his grandparents' bungalow. 'I'm beside the farm more or less, only a short walk down the road from the home place.'

'My father won't retire. He'll always be involved to some degree,' Edward adds firmly. 'And I would never ask him, because my father left school when he was fifteen, back in the day when it was the Inter Cert, and he took over the farm when he was seventeen.'

So for now, he is in a farm partnership with his parents.

Gordon Peppard, from Teagasc, was also born and reared on a farm in Wexford, in his case in Ferns. 'It was a small family farm … we had sheep and potatoes and cereal. We spent all our summers picking potatoes and selling them to the local shops and local people. Five of us were reared on it.'

Gordon was also the oldest son, but when he graduated at twenty-two his father was only fifty, far too young to retire. 'He wasn't going to step back at that stage, so I had to go off and get other work.' Farm partnerships did not exist at the time, so that was not an option. He eventually moved to Kilkenny, built a life there and had a family. He describes helping out on the farm when he goes home, now run by another younger sibling.

Does he miss it? I ask.

'Aw sure look it's born and bred into me, and I'd love to be farming I suppose.'

Farm partnerships registered by the Department of Agriculture are a farm business structure acknowledged by Revenue, Gordon explains. While they can be between those who are not related, in the main they tend to take place between family members, for example, a father or mother going into partnership with a son or daughter.

There are benefits for both sides with this arrangement. The older farmer might be, as Gordon says, 'too young to actually physically hand over the land, because hopefully he has a long number of days to live himself. He may have other kids himself in the family to educate, mortgages or bills to pay, so it's very difficult for him to hand over the farm at this point in his career.' They need to plan for the future, create extra hands on the farm and allow themselves a little more work/life balance.

For the younger person involved in the partnership, when a farm partnership works properly, 'they're on the bank account, on the herd number, part of the management decisions. And he has a profit-share ratio in the business. It gives the young person a standing rather than following Daddy around the yard, wondering will he ever get paid, will he ever be part of the business. The parent can go away for weekends, he can go to a wedding, go for a holiday, safe in the knowledge that the farm is running as normal. And it removes rural isolation.'

Registered farm partnerships evolved roughly twenty years ago. 'I suppose the need arose out of the lack of availability or access to land for young people,' Gordon explains. 'And out of the lack of sufficient labour or help for dairy farmers, without bringing in a person with some standing in the business. There's a lot of sentiment on Irish farms, and no one likes to give up the land.'

I was told stories of situations where a partnership ostensibly seemed to be in place, but in reality the older farmer refused to relinquish any of the decision-making power to the younger partner, and they were forced to kick their heels on any changes they wished to instigate about the running of the farm. In some cases, this resulted in the younger partner reaching an age where energy became an issue, because by the time they truly had a hand in running the place (when the older famer had passed away), they no longer had the stamina to enact much change.

The farm partnership on Edward's family's farm works well because the mindset is that of a collective, rather than an individual. At weekends Edward and his father work together on big jobs. During the week the son does what he can before and after his office job. 'I'd be up at six o'clock in the morning, I'd do an hour's checking then, usually the sheep around the block of land at the house. Then Daddy will go off down the lower land, and I'd go to work. In the evenings, it would be just various odd jobs: fixing something that might need to be done. I'm sort of a handyman, in that I'm an electrician, I'm a plumber, you know, welding – I'm very fortunate. Daddy was very hands-on, so he'd always have taught us everything. I always wanted that life. I'd happily give up my Monday-to-Friday job and farm all the time.'

For Edward, the lifestyle afforded by a farm is second to none: being outdoors, the simplicity of it, the variety of tasks, the range of environments. 'People nowadays live a fast pace, and it's all tech. The pace in here is a hundred miles an hour, 24/7, seven days a week,' he says of his day-to-day workplace. 'I have a company phone, I could be on at ten, eleven o'clock tonight, if there's issues with manufacturing. On the fields, you might be out fencing or moving sheep in a field, you can stop for five or ten minutes and just take in the scenery. The environment, the peace and quiet that you don't get when you're in a town, it's something you can't just put into words. Your own headspace. Living out in the countryside, there's such a magical feeling from it.'

Farming is 24/7 too, he acknowledges, but it is an entirely different pace. He's not buying the notion that farming is all-consuming, to the detriment of life beyond.

'I'm very much of the opinion that farmers were their own worst enemy for a good long time in saying "oh you can't switch off". You can make plenty of time for yourself. There are certain times in the year where you can be massively busy. At home on our farm, March and April are our mental months because we're at the peak of lambing. It's a lot of new life coming on the farm, a lot of extra work. But the rest of the year you can make ample time.'

Organisation is key, he says. 'Of course you're not going to go at a busy time on the farm, spring or harvest, but in every farming system there's quiet periods in the year. You can get windows of opportunity to get away, to switch off as well. There's a bit of an onus on the individual to take responsibility, to make that time for themselves too.'

'I always think it's a bit of ... guys that go along with that can't switch off, it's just pulling a shutter up. It's nearly the easiest option to do instead of making that time.'

I speak to a woman married to a farmer for decades now. Her husband has, by the sounds of things, pulled up the shutters. Their four children are raised, and she is in the phase of life where there is time again for friends, a social life beyond her children. Her husband is being left behind, however, unwilling to engage in anything beyond the farm. 'Some I think are just narrow-minded, they haven't gone past the farm gate or county border in years, they just can't think any further than the farm.'

Of her own husband, she says, 'if he had broadened his horizons, he would have a totally different outlook on life. I do think they can leave the farm if they want to, but sometimes it just comes up as an excuse. Say if years ago when we might have been invited to a wedding or something, the whole good is taken out of the day before you go, because suddenly a bit of fencing has to be done, or he would say I can't possibly go until this is done, so you're running on the last leg, you're wondering if you're going to get to the church part of the wedding at all. It's an awful lot about the discipline of themselves ... they can do an awful lot more than they think they can. I have my own job now, so I can finance myself in anything I want to do. I would be mixing with a lot more people now, and I'm sort of seeing that he's sat here on his own every evening in front of the TV talking to nobody. It's nearly as if his head is closed down to everything that's going on around him altogether.'

The marriage is over, but they are still living together in the house on the farm. 'His ultimatum is that if he leaves and finds somewhere else to live, then he can keep the farm. And if he doesn't I'm going to get it valued and split it.' In reality, she would never do this to their children, one of whom will take over the farm eventually.

So for now, they are at a dreadful stalemate. 'It is the farm that is holding it up. If it was just a house involved, I would have moved on years ago. I don't think he's ever going anywhere. He would be completely lost.' Despite not being on great terms with each other his clean washing is still in the cupboard, there's food always in the fridge. 'I'm moving forward and he's not. It's backwards he's going.'

Edward has been with his girlfriend for almost a year when we talk. They worked together for four years, but only got to know each other properly in the few weeks before she left the company where he still works. Their first date was a Sunday hike up Croghan Hill, just as friends, to see how they'd find each other's company.

'We'd talked as work colleagues, but we didn't really know anything about each other.' They brought a flask of tea and sat talking.

'The first little funny thing was when we poured out our tea, we both left our teabags in the cups. We both like strong tea,' Edward says with a laugh. 'It was the start of it, little simple things like that. We always laugh now when we go somewhere and people say, "Oh d'you want your teabag left in or out?" and we say, "Oh no, we both want it left in."'

They saw each other again the following Sunday, and the weekend after went for the legendary lunch in Kelly's Hotel. As they finished up, his now girlfriend said, 'Mammy's up home, d'you want to come meet her?'

'It's only the second weekend now, are you sure?' Ed replied, grinning now as he tells me.

'"Yeah. I kind of want to see how Mammy gets on with ye," she replied. Next thing we were up at her mother's for tea. She hadn't even told her that we were going,' he says, laughing again. 'She literally dropped me in it.'

He speculates that maybe it's the age they're at, early to mid-thirties, that allowed them to move relatively fast in terms of getting the relationship underway. They knew what they wanted.

'We've kind of always said we're not twenty-year-olds starting a relationship. We've both been in relationships. We know what we're looking for. The walk up Croghan Hill, we talked so much in those three hours it literally felt like we'd known each other for years and years, even though we'd never spoken properly before. There were so many connections. Similar interests in terms of nature and birds, we both have a fascination for robins. Little specific things, that you'd nearly think we were the carbon copy at times of each other. We just gelled so well with it.'

Meeting during restrictions, and travelling to see each other, their dates were all sober. 'It makes you have to talk more,' Edward says.

After visiting his girlfriend's mother, he suggested that as it was a bank holiday she might as well meet his parents. 'Sure, we've done your mammy now, you might as well come up home on the Monday. Sure, she was up home then on the Monday, met my parents.' He chuckles with delight at the memory.

Before meeting his girlfriend, Edward had had a relationship in his early twenties, then a few years of being single – 'I kind of pushed my career for a bit during that period'

– with nothing serious. The shift work he was doing at the time worked well for farming, but not for his personal life. 'Once I sat down in a chair, I would be just nodding off like.'

Aged twenty-nine, he joined online dating agency Elite Singles.

'At the time, what appealed to me was it was seen as being for the more-mature-mindset sort of person. I never joined Tinder or anything, because to me, Tinder serves one kind of purpose. Now I know there's couples who met on Tinder, and that's grand.'

Through Elite he met a woman from a neighbouring county. She found it difficult that Ed couldn't get away for a day, he recalls. At the time it was one of his busiest periods.

'I think we had gone out two Saturday evenings. We were talking really well and all. But the following weekend, we were shearing on the farm and I said to her, "I'm going to be honest with ya, I can't meet up next weekend because I'm going to be working from nine o'clock to maybe ten o'clock that night." Literally those two days, you do so much walking, you do 35,000 steps a day no bother, and I told her, "I'll be wrecked, and I'll just want to sit down, because I'll be going again on the Sunday." Because it takes a day and a half to shear all the sheep at home.'

You could see by her, Edward recalls, that she just wasn't getting it. '"But the guys are doing the shearing for ya?" I said I've to be there for organising, for making sure the right sheep go back to the right places. That was kind of the start of the end, when I look back on it.'

His current partner, while not a farmer herself, under-stands the demands of farming: her grandparents were farmers, and she grew up on a farm. It's something that comes up again and again: the need for a partner with an understanding for – and appreciation of – the rhythms of the lifestyle of farming, good and bad. It is important that a partner understands the relentless periods, but also has a yen for a life focused around the outdoors. 'She has a rural connection, if you know what I mean. She gets that at times something can pop up on a farm unforeseen, and plans can change. She understands sileage season. That it all comes, and those few days when we're cutting sileage that's all that matters, because we have to get the feed in right, we need it preserved well for the winter.'

His girlfriend has the openness to be able to know these things are part of life, and to look at the bigger picture and say, 'Oh okay, these few days are going to be hectic, I'm not going to see him, but overall, in the grand scheme of the thing, we will get that time together,' Edward explains. 'I'm very fortunate with my girlfriend that way, she understands that.'

She also shares his appreciation for the place in which he grew up. 'I find it hard sometimes to describe what the draw, the attraction is. Yesterday evening, after going around checking the sheep in the fields and around the house I came back into the yard and the sun was going down and shining in through the garden, reflecting across the different greens, and it's just so nice. You can't buy them moments. You can't put a price on them, that way of life. There's an inner connection in your gut that draws you to the whole outside. It's kind of, I'm not trying to sound hippy or anything, but it's just that connection to earth that really resonates with people of farming or agriculture.'

It's a pace and a way of life that both he and his girlfriend enjoy. 'You've a greater tendency to be on your own at times and enjoy your own peace and thoughts. We'd probably see each other four or five times a week now at the minute,' he smiles. 'On the evenings where we're not together, we'd be off walking separately, she could be walking the strand or something, I'd be home. Next thing, you're ringing each other, but you'd be out doing nearly the same thing, even if you weren't together.'

Part Two
Blow-Ins

7

I Was the Last to Know

The islanders knew that Paula's relationship was over before she did. She suspected as much, knew deep down really but ignored her suspicions. 'He had already moved on to somebody on the other island,' she tells me now, as we sit over the tea and breakfast she has made us in the kitchen of her home on a beautiful island off the Irish coast.

'I was the last person to know. He married six months later, and they have a baby now and another one on the way. Everyone knew before I did, because it was islanders over there who had seen him with her.' She started getting phone calls in the night from people, telling her what he was doing.

It was awful, she says now. Things were coming to an end, but she had kept the demise of the relationship to herself, and now for it to escalate and blow up as it did, 'I was mortified, the fact that it was so public. Even though I had done nothing wrong. But I suppose it's hard to be a private person in a small community like this at the best of times. I was embarrassed. It was just the fact that everybody knew. You're going through a break-up, you try to do it as privately as possible. You tell very few people.'

But then something began to happen. Remembering it, her voice cracks with emotion.

Now fifty-two, Paula, who grew up in Dublin, has lived on the island for ten years. An exceptionally warm, friendly person, she runs the shop and the post office for a local couple, a role that places her at the very centre of her small island community.

The islanders began to arrive at her place of work with gifts.

'The community here … people, started to give me presents. Little vouchers and cards, just to cheer me up. They'd come in and they'd hand you something and say, "That's for you, and we hope you stay"' – she slides an imaginary gift discreetly across the table, pats it.

It wasn't the first time she had experienced the community's support. When her beloved father had died six months before her relationship ended, *every* islander had sent her mother a card, even though many of them had never met her. Even now, almost three years on, they will still ask, 'how is your mother getting on?'

Several months after the break-up, her mother came to visit, and forced Paula to go out to the island's restaurant for dinner one night. Work was keeping her from going, but apart from that she had been struggling. 'I was a mess, I didn't want to get out of bed, I was on the sofa constantly.' Her mother told her briskly, 'Come on, get yourself into the shower and get dressed,' as mothers do.

'Mam I really don't want to go anywhere.'

'No, we're booked, we're going.'

They had a nice night, it was good to be out and dressed up, she recalls, 'and facing people again.' Afterwards, Paula went up to pay for their meal.

'That's paid for, Paula,' the owner told her.

'I said, "what d'you mean?"'

Her boss had called the restaurant and paid for the meal. The owner of the restaurant and the staff had paid for their drinks.

'I went back to our table and started crying. Mam said, "What's wrong with you now? Don't let that bastard get you down."' It's nothing to do with him, Paula sobbed back. She was overwhelmed at the kindness her community was showing her.

'I think what they thought was that I'd leave,' she says now. She did consider it. For one thing, she wasn't sure if she could afford to live as a single person, rather than in a couple. Could she do it on one wage, on her own? 'Do I, at forty-nine years of age, have to go back to live with my mother?' she had wondered.

Again, the islanders had stepped in with what she needed without being asked. Her bosses offered her a holiday home they usually let, giving it to her at a good rate, and gave her a raise. 'They all kind of made it possible for me to still live the life.'

Paula had always fancied a quieter life, always liked the idea of rural living, but never thought she would get the opportunity. 'This is *extreme* rural living,' she laughs.

When she was nineteen, she had visited another island. 'At that time there were no streetlights, the priest was on the door at the ceili that night checking for drink in your handbags. I remember thinking this place is fucking *amazing*,' she beams. 'There's just something magical about it. Never dreaming that I could have a life like that.'

Then you just get on with life, get a job, 'go through one disastrous relationship after the other.' Turning forty changed a lot, she says. She and a friend met some people from where she lives now at a wedding in Dublin and promised they would come visit, which they did a couple of months later.

'I just fell in love with the place. And that was in the depths of winter. There was just a wildness to it.'

People often talk about taking a year to adjust to the different pace of life when they move to a more rural area. Paula took to it immediately.

'I *always* wanted a life like that. Sitting on the M1 every morning stuck in traffic going to work, I don't miss that,' she shrugs. Paula hadn't planned on working that summer, she was on holiday, but when her bosses asked if she would do a few shifts, she obliged.

Before she came to live on the island, she had visited for weekends, and can see now that she did have a good sense of what it would be like to live there. 'It's not for everybody. Especially with here, there's no in-between, you either love it or you hate it. There's no stress. Just look out the window. My job has the same view,' she gestures proudly at the terraces of grey rock followed by the ocean visible from the window set into her front door.

At forty she found herself thinking, 'I want the rest of my life to be for me.' Everyone told her she was mad to move. 'What's wrong with you? Sure you can come back after a few weeks if it doesn't work out.' She thinks it's because it was such a different thing to do. 'Some people don't like change. All my friends were married by their early thirties, I never wanted to be married, young and tied down to that. I wanted to live. Not that married people don't live, but I wanted to live life on my own terms. And part of that was me moving here.'

When she first moved to the island, she hadn't given any consideration to how it would affect her chances of meeting someone. 'That didn't come into the equation at all. I just came here because it was what *I* wanted to do, for me.'

She met her ex-boyfriend six months after arriving. 'Dates?' she laughs gently at the notion I've suggested. 'You'd have to leave the island for that. We spent a lot of time in Dublin, stuff like that, to do something different. You can go to the pub here, go for a walk, but that's all you can do.'

Had they not met she thinks she may not have stayed on. 'I didn't think I could sustain a life here. I suppose the relationship kind of helped, and I'm not sure would I have lasted as long had I not met him. Which I think I would have regretted, because now, I'm in such a good place myself.'

The island is affordable, which means she can live on her own. That has become even more important over the years. 'I'll be fifty-two in June. I'm not ever going to get a mortgage. I'm not going to be able to afford to rent unless it's rural. On one wage, it's not affordable to go back to Dublin. I don't want to go back to Dublin anyway. If I ever had to move on from here, it would be to Connemara.'

It took a bit of getting used to, living as a single woman on the island rather than in a couple – another level of isolation. Again, her community sustained her. 'That first winter, I won't lie, it was lonely, and it was tough. But the group of friends I have here is amazing, everybody did everything in their power to keep me here. From there on I just turned the corner, joined the swimming group, kept plodding along.'

Now she is more content than she has ever been. Going through the break-up two years before we talk but, more importantly, losing her dad – the 'most important' man in her life – six months before that, completely changed her focus in life. It taught her to look after herself better than she had been doing.

Of late, she has tried online dating via a subscription with Match.com. She finds it 'hardcore. I can't cope with it', she laughs and rolls her eyes. 'The hardest part is trying to trawl through the shit. Who's genuine, who's not.'

She tells men she lives in the middle of nowhere. So far, she's given her number to three men, doesn't mind handing it out, 'it can be blocked at any point anyway.' It has not gone well.

There was a man to whom she gave her number. They were texting for a while when he wanted to video call.

'We video-called. He was only in his twenties, not thirty-nine as he'd said. And he was completely stark naked in the bed. Now, I pissed myself laughing. He's sitting with his dick in his hand. I swear to god. "Love. Put it away. Nobody wants to fucking see it."'

There was another one who said he was forty-four. When she gave him her number as requested, he immediately wrote back, *Is this for my father? He's into the auld ones.* 'I went, *Oh right, yeah, ha ha, lovely, hilarious.* And was just getting ready to block him when he sent another message: *How's your stamina for your age?* I sent back as quick as a flash, *Ask your father.* And blocked. What is the point of that? I don't know if it's a little ego boost, or they think they're funny. I'm thinking Jesus Christ, is this what it's like all the time.'

Her subscription ends the week we talk. She doesn't renew it. 'Too much hard work.'

What made her decide to try in the first place, I ask?

'I think I'm at a stage where, you know, maybe it would be nice to meet somebody, even though ultimately I'm very content with my life as it is. Since that relationship broke up I think I've become the person I was supposed to be, living where I'm supposed to live. I'm thinking about getting older as well, and do I want to die here a spinster? Part of me thinks well that would be alright – not everybody meets the love of their life. But the other part of that is, if it happens it happens. But if it doesn't it doesn't. I just thought I'd put myself out there a little bit. But with the online dating, I'm not enjoying it. It should be fun.'

She is not the best traveller, which means in the winter she won't get on the boat if the winds are too high.

'Islanders will tell you that you have to get off the island at least every six weeks. For your sanity. Get out, get to the real world, do normal stuff. But I don't miss normal stuff.' She once did a spell of not leaving for six months, and she was grand. 'Because I'm working all the time, that keeps me sane. And the swimming. I suppose at my age, it's the little things that keep you happy now. I don't need to be going to big shopping centres, there's nothing here that can't be got online. I don't need to be sitting in traffic every morning. There are times when I would like to be closer to my family, but they accept that this is the life I have chosen. They all originally thought I was cracked, and I'd be running home with my tail between my legs after two months.' Now they come to visit her every year with her nieces and nephews, and they tell her they get it. 'When Dad died, it was heartbreaking to come back then. I hated leaving my family,' she adds.

Will she stay? 'I suppose never say never, but probably not. There are days when you'd swim to the mainland to get out of here, but also days when I wouldn't want to be anywhere else.' She laughs. 'At the moment I'm the happiest I've been in many years.'

She enjoys her own company, crucial for living on the island, she says.

'There are nights you would be lonely, but you could be living in a city of 20,000 people and you could be just as lonely. It's all relative. I think there's a lot of pressure on people today to find someone to complete their life, their happiness, instead of finding it in yourself, which is much more important. I'm happy with where I am at the moment.'

8

Love at First Sight

The first time Aoife came to Connemara she was a teen-ager and visiting a friend from boarding school. From that first trip she felt an instant familiarity with the landscape: it reminded her of the desert in Saudi Arabia where she had grown up and where her parents still lived. 'It was love at first sight. It's got this kind of beauty where at first you might think it's barren but actually it's full of incredible life and nature and beauty.'

It's awe-inspiring, she adds. 'I find that power of nature incredibly grounding. It's bigger than everything, and it really helps take me out of my busy brain and into the moment.'

When her marriage ended in late 2019, Aoife needed to get out of Dublin where she had lived for some time. She again went west, to visit the old friend and her family in Clifden who by then she had been coming to stay with for over twenty years. When they offered her their rental

apartment in the centre of town for a few weeks, she immediately took them up on the suggestion.

Clifden was a place where she would come and feel
renewed. Five days into her stay, she decided this was where
she was meant to be and began looking for a place to live
long term. The plan was, she says with her wry smile, to take
the month of January off, process the ending of her marriage,
and that would be job done. She would be ready to move on.
'Then I can go back to work, right?' she says briskly, then
laughs at herself and at the bargains we try to make with
grief, our imagined sense of being able to control its passage.
It soon began to dawn on her that it was 'going to take a *little*
bit longer than that', she says with a smile.

In February 2020 Aoife spent a day moving into her
new flat with the help of her mum and sister.

'It felt like I was coming to a place that was very familiar.
Connemara for me creates space. There's less distraction, so
you have to face your shit. And actually, that is really difficult. At the wrong time you might struggle to come and
live in a place like this. I think it was wise of me at the time
to get a little flat in the town. It would have been too much
to be, "hey come to Connemara and be isolated in a little
farmhouse in the middle of the winter, and just have all of
your entire emotional history to wade through"'.

Instead, being in town, but having direct access to the
'epic nature' of the place, provided just the right balance.
'It was exactly what I needed at that time.'

And then the pandemic started, forcing her to really
stop. Rather than living the life she had imagined, based
in Connemara but travelling each week to her work with

the Sing Along Social, she was suddenly grounded entirely and cut off from the few friends she already had in the remote area she had *just* moved to.

Despite this, the first few months of lockdown were fine. At times even fantastic. 'Basically, I was on a one-woman retreat. I had a two-hour bath every morning, it was just me and my dog, I got to walk her every day, I was *extremely* moisturised, like hydrated, exfoliated, moisturised. I slept so much.'

The very geography of her new place felt protective. 'I can't describe how at home and held I felt. I guess it's like being around a loved one. I feel safe and seen and heard, but also really excited to get to know them even more,' she says of her home.

'From the beach you could see the Twelve Bens,' she says, describing the mountain range that runs throughout the centre and north of Connemara. 'I could also see them from my flat window. So many times when I was in lockdown, totally isolated, by myself, and something from my past might come up – if I was worrying, or feeling anxious, or ruminating – I would use the mountains as a barrier. *That belongs over there. You're here now. You're safe.'* They were a 'protective forcefield', she says.

She had come from an extremely high-energy, stimulating job running The Sing Along Social – what she calls 'a zero-commitment choir designed for people who cannot sing' – which appears at festivals, regular residencies and private events. Now there was a complete change of pace. It turned out it was exactly what she needed. Over the past few years Aoife has lost a really dear friend to cancer and

experienced the breakup of her marriage. 'In one way having a busy, joy-filled job really got me through it. But I
think it was also really difficult, because when you're feeling very, very, very sad, and you have to reach a happy
place for work, it takes a lot of energy.'

Now she knew she needed to be quiet. 'It was kind
of like how wounded animals go and hide. I think animals have an instinct to go somewhere that they feel
safe. And that's how I would describe it: I was a little
animal, I was *really* wounded. And I just went to a place
where I felt safe.'

It was difficult, though, having moved to an already isolated place and being cut off from the small network that had
made Clifden seem so hospitable in the first place. Maybe it
was, in part, being there but cut off from most of Connemara
at the same time that made it so difficult, she reflects. She
could see it, but couldn't get out into it when we were in our
most extreme lockdown.

Ironically, when things began to open up and she was
able to see the friends she had missed so much, Aoife found
herself struggling, unable to connect with people. She
missed her work which, under restrictions at the time, was
still not possible.

As the reopening of society progressed in the summer
of 2020, Aoife went to her GP. 'Because it was so fucking
difficult. All of this grief, all of that pain. The loneliness. All
the terrible things that were going around in my head.'

She was linked into mental health services. Group
therapy was not available because of the pandemic.
Instead, she had a weekly phone session with a HSE

therapist – for six months they talked every week. The therapist gave her tools and strategies which were genuinely lifesaving, she says.

'I think I got incredibly lucky. It's something that, when you move to a rural place, you don't expect to be able to get access to *more* services. But like, maybe it was a combination of the pandemic, it was also certainly my age, my privilege, my ability to advocate for myself.'

The therapy became a process of investigating different parts of herself. That, and being in Connemara, 'just supported me in having space to get to know myself properly, and to really build self-trust,' she says of her surroundings. 'That's been a major thing. I think for years I didn't trust myself, my instincts, my gut. I think self-trust is something as women we struggle a lot with in our culture. It's definitely something that being queer, but not out myself, that was a huge part of it.'

In the summer of 2020 Aoife came out to family, friends, and then her community at large. 'It's kind of hard to explain but it's like I always knew that about myself, but I hid it because I was ashamed. Because society told me to be ashamed. When I stood up to that shame and proved that I could be happier living a more truthful life, that has helped me to trust myself more and more.'

When she was younger, Aoife had put her queerness aside, she says. 'You know, I was a teenager in the nineties, and you just have to watch *Friends* to see how homophobic the culture was. I was in a boarding school. I was thousands of miles away from my family, I was already a bit weird to be honest. And I had *just* been accepted by friends. I also liked men too. It became something that was harder to ignore as I got older. I would get very emotional hearing stories of queer people. There are many queer people in my close group of friends, and I would *totally* consider myself an ally. And then I realised that their needs or causes were so important to me because they were my own, and it made sense why it had meant so much to me over the years.'

Spring 2021 came, and the lease was up on her flat. She moved to her current home. Set slightly above the road, it looks out onto the water. It is a house of women, she smiles. She adores her flatmate and her landlady.

We sit in her living room, a beautiful room with an entire corner of glass walls. As we talk, the Connemara colours – browns, heathers, the dark grey of the sea – are our backdrop, the tones changing every few minutes as the light drops. Daffo, Aoife's dog, sits beside me, pride of place in her basket on the couch.

It felt like things were coming together in her new life in this new home. Then in March 2021, Aoife fell and broke her ankle. She was rescued by friends, she explains: in the immediate moment, by her old boarding-school friend, who came to find her on the beach and called the emergency services; then later, by another friend, who took her in for the last lockdown.

'They adopted me, essentially, for six weeks. That was recovery for my heart. To be a part of a family, to be a part of an "us", I felt I'll never be able to repay them for that. Again, everyone had retreated,' she says of what it was like to be single and living alone during lockdown. 'It really made me understand how isolated I had been.'

Aoife turned forty not long after we first met. When your marriage ends, it is very easy to think you will never meet anyone again. Aoife puts this in the context of not wanting to have a baby herself, that it took the pressure off meeting someone else. 'I have decided that I don't want to be pregnant, I don't think that's the right thing for me. What it means as a woman is that there wasn't the same urgency. The fact that I am a woman who doesn't want to bear children gives me the luxury of thinking wait until you're older, or don't worry.' That said, she was pretty convinced that she would be alone. 'I remember thinking, *This is it; I'm going to be alone, and that's okay. I've loads of friends, family, that'll be fine.*'

When we talk again, she tells me with a sweetly proud smile, that since she moved to Clifden, she has had three relationships with women who she met online via a dating app, through a chance encounter, and through an introduction by a mutual friend, respectively.

'Something I learned from my marriage ending is that just because something doesn't last forever doesn't mean it isn't a true, and good, and utterly worthwhile experience. It can be very painful to let go but perhaps that knowledge gives me a bit more freedom in moving through shorter-term but ultimately very meaningful relationships.'

'They're relationships that Connemara has given space for. I love the saying, "If you do things you like you'll meet people you like." I've been wondering, if I live in a place that I love, maybe I will meet people I love, you know? And that's been true for friendships, and it seems like it's true for romantic relationships as well.'

Being in Connemara – in a new place, starting a new life – leant a certain freedom to coming out. 'Freedom to meet women and have the feelings that I'd always had but had hidden. I think it was the space to think about it, and also I suppose it offered a certain amount of privacy as well. No one there has known me in a close relationship. Of course my close friends did, but yes, I think there's definitely that element … I suppose it's the cliché of going away and reinventing yourself. Only I don't think that I've reinvented myself, I've come into myself. I was able to step into being fully myself. It helped that lots of new people I was meeting didn't know me at all.'

Her coming out experience has been deeply supported by family, friends, and the people she lives amongst in Clifden, Aoife hastens to add. 'The reason for that is every single queer person before me who didn't have a good time coming out. Who it was difficult for, and the people who fought to change that.' It is still scary though, coming out. 'Because homophobia is still alive, it's still a threat. You're not guaranteed to be accepted.'

I wonder how it was in the more difficult times, after a breakup, during the darker moments of winter. Did she ever question the move, find it too lonely, too hard? In fact, Aoife speaks about her life in Connemara in terms of an immersive self-care experience.

'Connemara just happens to offer me the perfect ingredients for deep self-care. Part of something that can make our journeys as little easier is if we find the things that make our daily lives just a little bit better, easier, more supported.' For Aoife, life in Connemara does that.

'I think one of the mistakes we make when we think about self-care is that the same things work for everyone. Like *everyone* should be sea swimming. Loads of people are afraid of water, and loads of people don't like the cold. It does not work for everybody. In the same way that loads of people cannot stand the wet windy stormy days of Connemara, I absolutely adore them.'

She loves the wildness and the unpredictability of that weather. That the only thing that is guaranteed is that it will change. 'That is like the truth about life. That is the only certainty, that everything changes.'

She lists the things she loves about her home, the scenery, the sea swimming and the magical clear blue water, the hill walking she's just gotten into, although she calls it 'ambling upwards', her supportive flatmates, and Daffo, who also loves Connemara. 'It's a really strong foundation on which to build the rest of my life.'

It's coming to the end of our time together, and we decide to go for a walk by the sea, driving up over a swell in the Sky Road, the beaches spread out below us, the water reflecting the pattern of the sky.

Aoife's story feels full of transition and change. Does she think being in Connemara created momentum for transformation? 'I think sometimes to change, or transform we have to know ourselves. And to feel grounded in that knowing of ourselves. There's something about Connemara, from the first moment I saw it as a teenager, I felt at home here. I felt that I knew it. There's something about the place, and the constant change in the weather and the landscape, that gives me perspective on how everything really does change and evolve constantly, all the time every day. Without realising, it may have been a very supportive backdrop for that.'

Will she stay? I ask as we walk up a sand dune. She looks at me kindly but as if to say we both know that that is silly question.

'Oh yes,' she smiles, throwing the ball again for Daffo.

9

Pen Pals

When she first moved to her new town, Trini was careful about dating.

Trini is used to moving. When she was eight, her family moved from Dublin to Australia. Since moving back to Ireland, she has lived in Dublin, Galway, Limerick and then Ardagh. Now, aged forty-one, she has moved to Newcastle West in County Limerick, the population of which is around 6,000.

This latest move was professionally motivated. When she last relocated, she was entirely focused on work. Having been out of her career for a long time, and now that she was back on track, she wanted to do her best. 'I think maybe I was putting excessive boundaries on myself. I was trying to be really strict with myself and to do a really good job.'

I have to be professional, she recalls thinking. Hers is a community development role with funding aspects, which means lots of engagement with local businesses. It's not that it's political, she says of her work, but there *are* small-town politics. She was worried she might say the wrong thing – looking back, she was maybe *somewhat* paranoid, she says. 'Also, on the dating side of things, if you don't know anyone and you don't know who you're talking to … I've been picked up in a bar many a time,' she laughs. What if, without her knowing it, someone saw her chatting to their husband, a man she did not realised was married? She therefore found herself placing restrictions on her own behaviour.

Usually, she would have no problem going into a bar anywhere in the world, sitting down and chatting to anyone. Now she felt she had to behave differently, what she describes as putting a barrier on herself. 'I don't want to sit next to the wrong person and say the wrong thing about one of my work projects,' she recalls thinking. 'They might be professionally involved with one of the projects I was working on, or maybe in the future they'd be involved in one.' Now that she is more settled in her job, this has changed.

We're sitting in the apartment she rents with a friend in the centre of the town, the river visible from the open window. She has been single for 'seven solid years', she tells me, after splitting with her boyfriend in 2013. Since then, the maximum she has dated a man is for a couple of months.

When she dated in Galway, it was rebound dating. This move, to Newcastle West, was for professional reasons – it changes how you date, Trini explains. She recalls talking to a man online one night after she made the move to where she now lives. He told a joke she didn't have a response to, didn't particularly like, and she let the conversation go. The next day she walked into a car dealership. 'He was the guy selling me the car.'

'I was chatting to you last night,' she said.

'Oh were you? Ohhhh.'

'Our first and only date was the test drive of the car,' Trini – who is funny, blunt and direct in conversation – says dryly. Even if she hadn't liked his joke, she wouldn't have brought that any further anyway, she says, because of him living locally.

She tells me her theory on online dating apps, the pattern she has figured out with Snapchat, WhatsApp, Instagram. 'I've had one or two weirdos who have asked for Facebook. You're like, *hell no*. You sociopath–definitely not,' she chuckles.

'You've got guys that just want pen pals. They'll sit there and chat to you back and forth, but you'll never meet them. The *number* of guys who you'll never meet up with. I've started saying to them, "I don't want a pen pal." I'd say, like all of us, they want to just pass the time sometimes.' These sorts of exchanges tend to take place on WhatsApp.

'The ones who want to move to Snapchat – two messages in and you're getting a dick pic. Almost invariably.' Unsolicited, without warning? 'Almost invariably.'

'Once I figured out the pattern I was like, this guy has asked me for my Snapchat, do I *want* to see his dick?' Sometimes she'll think 'ah sure go on – depending on what level of inebriation, or hangover, or rebound I was currently on'.

'It notifies you if they do the screenshot,' she says of sending pictures back on Snapchat. 'And obviously no face.

But sure if you're bored, meh,' she shrugs. Those who contact you on Instagram just want a new follower.

Initially, Trini was on Tinder only. She set her filters for age and location wide although, until recently, never for anyone much older than her, 'because I just wouldn't be into them.'

The pool of people she is attracted to on dating apps has become 'noticeably' smaller as each move has brought her to a more compact community. Having criteria is important for online dating, she explains. You need some kind of filter, a checklist, to sort the wheat from the chaff. 'Not wanting to be judgemental or anything, but you have to kind of categorise people, you know? What do you do for a job? It's different if you meet people in person. But you have to have some criteria on the app, because otherwise you'd be trying to go on dates with everyone.'

She goes through periods of what she calls manic swiping, 'manic manifesting' she laughs, miming the swiping. 'Ah go on, ah go on. Where you would give a good few yeses. The only problem with that is that they do the same thing, so you'll get a load of matches, but then you have to go and trawl through them all.' She rolls her eyes at the work element involved in online dating, the sheer life admin of it.

To cut down on the load, she wrote a standard opening. *'Hey [name], how are things* … I copied and pasted it, and just changed the name. Two or three times I didn't change the name,' she chuckles dryly. 'Needless to say, *those* conversations did not go anywhere.'

She's on Bumble now. 'I'm not going back on Tinder again. Just no. Nobody's on Tinder to meet a potential partner.' Recently, she started to reconsider the age of the men she was swiping on, feeling that she might be limiting herself. 'Why wouldn't I go for somebody forty to forty-five? I extended my setting there.'

And she began to wonder if she had changed her mind about wanting children. 'I was *actively* not having kids for all of my twenties. Then all of my thirties were *actively* avoiding a relationship, and going out with younger guys, because I didn't think that it was something that I wanted.'

Covid-19 has changed her mindset. The loneliness was dreadful. She was mostly living on her own and unable to travel, a thing she would have relied upon previously. 'Part of my commitment issues were that I wanted to be transient, I didn't want to be stuck anywhere.'

As restrictions came into place and everyone retreated into their family units, for those living on their own – cut off from whatever network they had created outside of the home – it was particularly isolating.

'Seeing how my friends did it with their kids, that kind of family support unit when the world is so uncertain,' Trini recalls. She had never needed people like that before, because *she* had made certainty in her life, she says. 'If I didn't like something, I'd move. And I couldn't do that anymore.'

She began to wonder how much of her behaviour was a fear of commitment or of settling down. 'How many nice guys have I shut down, yet I'll keep chatting to the guy who sends dick picks?' She rolls her eyes. 'How much of that is a fear of getting trapped, of getting stuck?'

She had never wanted children but began to question that. Was a decision made in her twenties still the right decision? 'I'm letting 25-year-old me dictate how things will be for me as a fifty-year-old, a sixty-year-old, a seventy-year-old. And that's not fair.'

She watched friends embarking on fertility treatment or realise that it was too late for them to have children, and it made her wonder. Then she looks at the lives of friends with kids and thinks pfft, not sure of that either.

Being so isolated for the past two years has made her rethink everything.

'Only because of Covid-19, I would not have had any fear or worry otherwise. But now it's like, I want to know that I've given myself that opportunity. I didn't really know anything beyond only staying somewhere for a couple of years. But I decided I wanted to change that.'

When we met first, Trini was looking to buy a house in the area. Several months later, she purchased her own home. 'It was honestly just everything came together,' she says of what finally decided her on a place, after all the restless moving. 'There's nothing specific about Newcastle West.'

She was in her job long enough that she could afford a mortgage. At first, she did consider living somewhere totally isolated.

'Thinking right, I'm really going to dig deep, move on to the top of a mountain, really isolated, but they were all really run down. I believe in magic and the universe and it just telling ya where you're going to be. This place came up. In fairness I am not on the top of a mountain, I'm just in the middle of the town. It came up, and I was ready. Not even that I was ready to buy, I was ready to stop moving.' Now, she spends her time off slowly beginning to create a home of her own. For the moment, Trini is not dating.

10

Go on a Date And
Drive for Five Hours

Graham moved out of the family home in County Louth when he was sixteen. The youngest of several brothers, he had just come out. His family is quite Catholic, he says, and at the time were still 'a bit strange with the gay thing', he recalls, so Graham left, 'to give them kind of time to adjust to it.' He moved to Dublin, where he ended up getting a job in a restaurant, lying about his age. ('Are you going to fire me?' the teenager asked his boss when she found out. She gave him day shifts instead and kept a protective eye on him.)

At the age of twenty-four Graham was diagnosed with HIV. 'That was a big shock to my system. I wanted to change my lifestyle in some way. It didn't come from my lifestyle, what happened, but I felt like I wanted to get away from the city then.'

'When it comes to dating, I find it important to disclose my status early in the conversation. The main reason is I don't want to wait two weeks of chatting to find out if the guy is uncomfortable about it. Things are improving but there are still a lot of guys that would see me as unclean, or dirty. Over the years, guys have blocked me immediately after I tell them. There is a lot of judgement, but nowadays I chat to more guys who are better educated and more accepting.'

Graham is dark-haired and strikingly handsome. Now thirty-two, he speaks in a low, gentle voice – his tone barely changes even when he recounts the more dramatic parts of his story.

After his diagnosis, he decided he wanted to get out of the city. He moved to the French Alps, the work was outdoors and he loved it, 'the nature and the animals, everything about being in the countryside.'

He loved learning about how a smaller community did things, which felt entirely different to what he had known growing up. But seven months after he arrived Graham was hit by a drunk driver, who left him lying in the snow in minus temperatures. It was two hours before he was found and brought to hospital. Both of his legs were broken, and his face was badly injured.

'I got my surgery, so I'm all titanium from the knees down now,' Graham says. He returned to his parents' house to learn to walk, spending about a year there getting himself back up on his feet. His mother told him how proud she was of him, for surviving, and getting back out in the world. 'Getting hit by a car helped our relationship. I would never have chosen to move back to my parents' house at the age of twenty-five, otherwise. It was a nice part of my life, to be cared for by my parents at that age. They would talk about me very proudly now.'

As soon as he was fully mobile again, he had 'a kind of longing to get back out into the wild'. This time, he went to Iceland, where he spent three years, most of it in the remote Westfjords.

When his relationship there ended, he returned to Ireland, now with two dogs in tow, Alaskan Malamutes. It wasn't that he was especially drawn to the west, he smiles, rather Connemara was the only place he could afford to live that had a pet-friendly house. He moved to Lettermullan, a place in ways even more remote than where he now lives, he laughs.

He felt free and independent, he says of the move. His previous relationship had become difficult. Connemara provided a kind of refuge. 'I was happy with whatever life I had in Connemara because I got away from a bad situation. That was all that mattered at the time. I was setting up my own life somewhere far away for my ex-boyfriend.' The move rendered his love life non-existent. He might get chatting to someone on a dating app, but as soon as they heard where he lived, they would have no interest.

'*What are you doing out there like?* From Galway it was an hour-and-a-half journey, so just to go for a day you're talking about a good bit of travelling. I would understand where they were coming from.' He didn't want to move back to a city again though. After the accident in France, Graham was diagnosed with PTSD and found it difficult to be around crowds.

'I'm away from all of that in the peace and quiet where I am.' Two years ago, he moved to Inis Meáin. 'The same

119

as Connemara, but here on the island it's like everything is slowed down.' The remoteness of where he is provides a sense of safety.

'I have felt very like I'm in a refuge over here. Especially here on the island, because when I was in Connemara, my ex would have sent me messages every now and again. He wanted to take one of the dogs back from me.'

Graham was worried that his ex might confront him about the dog, but knew that the community would fore-warn him if he ever decided to show up. (He had only one dog by this point, having re-homed one as the two together had become unmanageable.)

He moved from Connemara after spotting an ad for a job in the knitting factory where he now works.

'I sent an email to them and said I don't really have any experience in the marketing job, but if you have anything else, like something manual, I'd be pretty good with my hands and stuff.' He told them he thought he would do well living on the island, that he had previ-ous experience of being in a remote community. 'I think they take that on board in these kinds of places. They contacted me almost immediately and brought me over for an interview.'

They warned him that it can be difficult, especially dur-ing the wintertime, but Graham, who says he likes his own company, had a good sense of what he was getting into. 'As long as they had a place that was affordable to rent with my dog, then I was happy. And then I can go places at the weekend. So that's kind of what got me the job, because I have no experience in knitwear. It's gone well.'

Just a few weeks before the first lockdown, Graham made the move. What's it like living in such a small community?

'The way I see it is, being from Dublin, I'm just as foreign as the Brazilian girl down the road, because I'm not an islander. And if you're not an islander you're a foreigner.'

A colleague in the knitting factory has worked there for the last thirty years, 'but he's always going to be Alan from Longford,' Graham laughs.

He has just come through his second winter and he found it harder than the first. 'It was pretty isolating the last few weeks. The islanders can be quite private, so if you're spending winter here, and you're living alone, you're spending the majority of it alone. I was struggling a few weeks ago.'

To help, he took a studio on the mainland to spend weekends in. He thought he might go into Galway more.

'But the studio was in Connemara. I was going there for a few weeks and sitting in the woods on my own, and so it didn't do anything for my loneliness. I was just moving to another place to be on my own,' he says. 'I'd rather be alone on the island. And then if I want to go off for the weekend, I can pay for a hotel somewhere.'

Graham has been on the apps consistently since he moved west. More just to talk, he explains, he doesn't meet people much.

For some, it's a novelty that he is 'making Aran jumpers on an island'. But it can be a conversation killer. 'At the end of the day, if somebody's over in Clare, and we're having a chat, we're only eleven miles apart, but like it'll take me two and half hours to get to them, and two and a half hours back. I don't even want to think about going on a date with someone and driving for five hours,' he laughs.

He has had a couple of summer romances. 'Maybe it's just a seasonal thing, like everything here, they don't come along until the summer.' In the summer months he would get messages from guys on the apps, do you want to meet up tonight. They are on Inis Mór, 'I'm not on your island,' he has to tell them.

Each time he comes back to asking himself: is this realistic? A guy from Tipperary who he met online came to the island for a date. They hiked and had a drink afterwards, 'had a lovely time'. But when a return visit was discussed it became clear that Graham's dog would not be welcome.

'I draw the line there,' he laughs. 'Because if I can't bring the dog then I can't come.' More than that though, when he begins to consider the logistics, things seem too difficult. 'There's only a ferry to Clare in the summer. So you'd have to drive from Connemara to Tipperary, to do that at the weekend, you'd get there, and it would be nearly time to go home, you know? I just told him I don't see how it would work.'

There was another guy who arrived on the island as part of a hiking holiday. He came back to visit, they got on well. Graham went to visit him for several weeks in Donegal. 'We had a really good click. But when I came back to the island, I'd only really known this guy for two weeks, so I was thinking where do we go from here? It's nearly a day travelling to get to each other. It's hard to find a happy medium. You need to get to know each other before one of you makes the drastic choice to move. But how to achieve that with such distance between you?'

'I only just know you, and I wouldn't be comfortable with having you move into my house,' explains Graham about his dilemma. 'And if things didn't work out, I don't want to be responsible. If I wanted to move to Donegal, I'd have to give up everything I have here to go there. And I never wanted to move to Donegal before, so that's why I said to him, "you're a lovely guy, but I don't want to do this back and forth for a couple of years to figure out if it's going to work or not". I'd prefer to be available for guys that are in Galway, for example, that I could probably meet more easily.' He's on Tinder and Grindr. Tinder you have to match with someone before they can contact you but Grindr is very instant. Everyone can see if you're online straightaway, and they can write you a message.'

Grindr, launched in early 2009, and aimed at gay and bisexual men, was one of the first of the geosocial dating apps, at the time a revolutionary concept. As a location-based app it allowed you to see where the nearest gay man was. Stephen Fry, who spoke about the app on *Top Gear* a few months after its launch, is often credited with really helping it to take off.

'Ninety per cent of the guys on Grindr want to talk about sex, and they'd be sending all sorts of pictures to me.' He feels indifferent about being sent nudes. 'I've had a Grindr profile for a decade, and it's so normal there … A part of my day is going to work and getting a dick in my phone, from somewhere, if I go online. A guy twice my age in Clare, sending me pictures of himself and expecting me to have a chat with him. I wouldn't feel violated, because it's gone on so long in the gay world. I guess I just ignore it. If I find it really disgusting, I block them in case they send any more.'

It is hard to find what he is looking for on the apps.

'I wouldn't be too interested, like, when they want to talk about sex. I couldn't be bothered. I think with a lot of gay men it's almost assumed that if you're online, that's what you're looking for. It is difficult because it almost feels emasculating to say, "well no, actually, I'm looking for a relationship. I'm looking for, like, flowers, or chocolates, that kind of thing,"' he laughs. He's moving from Grindr and Tinder to Hinge because he has heard it's more relationship orientated. He wants a monogamous relationship, a mindset he has found hard to come across. 'I don't feel attracted to other people when I'm in a relationship. I became kind of bitter about the whole thing, because I was like, what's the point? You're getting excited to go out and meet other people, I'm sitting here at home, with the dogs.'

The difficulty of meeting someone from his current home means he thinks his time on the island is finite. 'I don't want to be one of the auld fellas here who lives on their own, and they've always lived on their own, they've lived all their life as bachelors.' Sometimes the women here call him a bachelor, he laughs, 'as if I'm one of them. These guys are more than twice my age. I think, oh well no, no, we're not the same. I'm not in my seventies yet. I don't want to get to that point, and then look back at my life and think, well shit I wish I went and looked for love. It can seem like you're less of a catch if you live in the middle of nowhere.'

For the past two years the apps have felt like the only way of meeting someone. He wants to go to The Outing Festival, a music, matchmaking and queer arts festival, which began as part of the Lisdoonvarna Matchmaking Festival before moving to County Clare, but it has been cancelled for the past two years.

'But I think a lot of people are not having romance. Well, a lot of people that live in the country, anyway. I wouldn't see myself as any less deprived of sex than my friend up the road's who's a straight female.'

He doesn't feel like he has a sexuality on the island, he reflects. 'People have said to me a few times that they're very open here on the island, they don't care about your sexuality. And I said, "Well I'm not having sex with anyone on the island, so I don't have a sexuality." It's only when I go off the island that I'm gay. I'm not gay here, there's nobody to be gay with,' he smiles.

He has found the islanders very accepting. 'Wouldn't it be great if they got married here on the cliff. It would be our first gay marriage,' a neighbour said to a friend. 'Well he has to find himself a man.'

When he was living in rural Iceland with his boyfriend, he felt freer to be a little more flamboyant, he says thoughtfully. 'I think that they have accepted people for who they are a lot longer than we have. They're not religious, they have not been religious for generations. The three years I was there, the only time I came across someone who was a little bit uncomfortable with me and my sexuality was a foreigner.'

'Things have gone very trendy in the countryside in the last few years,' Graham smiles. 'They loved having a gay guy in Connemara where I was, for some reason, they thought it was brilliant. I think it would be the same here if I was to bring a guy back with me.'

He does feel detached from the gay community, something which makes him consider moving back to a city at times. 'I'm happy and content with my life here, but a few years ago when I was dating, I was happy with that life as well.' He thinks eventually he will move on.

11

Cinegael Paradiso

Betsy grew up on the east coast of America, and first came to Ireland when she was twenty-four. She met her husband on a course in the Aran Islands and they eloped in 2013. Afterwards, the couple moved to East Galway, where he is from, and eventually had a child together – a little boy – but the marriage didn't work out. When it ended in 2018, Betsy stayed for a while where they had lived as a couple before moving, first to Inverin, then to Carraroe in Connemara, where she now lives with her four-year-old son.

For some time after the marriage ended, Betsy had no interest in dating. Loneliness didn't especially bother her. Much of her work has been solitary – she is an author now working on her sixth book and has always been a homebody. And she found herself enjoying being a single parent. Dating wasn't a priority. Her focus was on building a life and a home for herself and her son on her own terms.

'I think you do have to decide as a single parent which parts of your life are going to be on hold. It's going to be *something,*' she says. 'When my ex-husband and I broke up and it was incredibly traumatic and I didn't have a home, the thing that people would say to me was "oh don't worry, you'll find someone else". And I would think it's *literally* not what I'm worried about right now,' she laughs. 'I couldn't afford a hole in the wall in Galway city, so I knew I needed to live in a rural area to make ends meet.'

Carraroe, or *An Cheathru Rua* (the red quarter), is a village in Connemara set on a peninsula west of Galway city by about fifty kilometres, known for its distinctive traditional boat, the Galway hooker.

On the drive out to her house I pass the TG4 headquarters, something of a surprise of a building in amongst the repeated mix of 'Bungalow Bliss' houses, Costcutters and other small stores, schools, and signs saying 'AIRE PAISTI AG TREASA' that line either side of this part of the Wild Atlantic Way – or the road out to Spiddal, as it is known locally. Carraroe is in the heart of the Gaeltacht, the majority of its approximately 2,500 inhabitants are Irish speakers. Betsy is just beginning to learn the language, she says almost apologetically, it's something she feels a bit self-conscious about.

We talk on the phone a few times before I visit her in early January 2022. It's a freezing but golden day. Since just before the pandemic began, Betsy has been renting a building called the Old Knitting Factory, a property built by the Congested Districts Board in 1906 as a place where women could work and earn some money. A long, low building set just off the road between a rocky outcrop and Lake Mhuilinn, it doesn't look like a workplace, but rather a sizeable cottage.

It is thought some of the women who worked there used their wages to pay for their trip to America. Now Betsy, an American, lives there with her child.

In the 1970s the building was bought by the filmmaker Bob Quinn. As well as raising most of his six children in the then one-storey building (there is now a small upstairs room that Betsy and her boy use in the winter evenings. The high ceilings in the rest of the house make it hard to heat), he also ran a cinema, Cinegael, from the house, a story told by his son Robert Quinn in the documentary *Cinegael Paradiso*.

We sit over several pots of tea and a packet of Rich Tea biscuits in her kitchen, the light glinting back at us from the still water, Betsy's cat glaring indignantly at me from outside the full-length glass doors. The room has vaulted ceilings and one wall is exposed stone, decorated with colourful child's drawings.

After a year and a half of being separated and single, when she had just turned thirty-one, Betsy decided she was ready, not for a relationship but for a one-off interaction. It was partly just to aid the process of moving on, she explains.

There is no family network nearby to provide babysitting. As a self-employed single parent money is tight, so funds for babysitting were not plentiful. She relied mostly on friends, occasionally her childminder. Time is also tight, she points out – she would like to spend it with her child. But she decided she wanted to invest some of that time in dating, so joined some apps.

'The first two dates that I went on, friends came over after I had put my son to bed. I had told him that I was going out. I drove into Galway, had my date, and drove back.' Not drinking doesn't bother her, she says, smiling at the question. She's American, she is used to it.

Betsy is bisexual, and her first date was with a woman who suggested that they go to a group ukulele lesson in Galway city. 'That was a really good date. It was great because we weren't immediately having to keep up a conversation the whole time. We were just given uku-leles and we were learning. We could joke a bit, but we didn't have to have a whole big conversation. After that we walked to a bar together and had a good talk, it was lovely. It was great that she sort of took the lead on what to do. She was very nice, and we had a kiss at the end of the date.'

Online dating in the form of apps had not existed when Betsy met her husband, and this was not just her first date post-separation, but her first proper date ever with a woman.

'I had met women at parties, stuff like that. And I had been on OkCupid back in America, and listed myself as interested in men and woman, but the thing is, men are just so much more plentiful,' she laughs, putting her hand to her short hair and scrunching it. Betsy has pale pink hair, and translucent glasses of an even paler pink. Sometimes when she laughs there's an almost anxious quality to it. There's a diffident gentleness to her that is very moving.

Then, in Connemara, she began using Tinder and Bumble. The word 'cesspool' comes up more than once when people describe Tinder to me. Betsy is the third to use it. What struck her was – given that here she was specifically looking for just sex, which seemed to be what many of the men she encountered on Tinder were also looking for–how often those men bungled it for themselves.

'I was there because I wanted to go on dates. I had been married, and then I had been with *no one* for like a year and a half, so I really wanted to sleep with someone,' she laughs. 'Like, that was a goal of mine.'

She describes how men got in the way of achieving that goal. 'It's really funny to me, because there were so many men who I thought were attractive, and it would not have been hard for them to get me to sleep with them, but they messed it up for themselves so quickly by just being really crude, and demanding sex immediately.'

She set her bar low, she smiles wryly. Just one civilised exchange was all she was looking for.

'If they had had one conversation with me, like just be a decent person for *one* day, they would have gotten what they wanted. I wasn't looking for a commitment or anything. It was fascinating to me how many men would shoot themselves in the foot by being really explicit right away, and wanting to send you pictures of their penis, or asking you all these weird sexual questions. Like, all they have to do is just be nice, for a short period of time.'

She suggests that online interactions allow people to be bolder than they would be in real life. 'Certainly I think that there are a lot of men on the internet who would be mortified if their mother found out the kinds of things that they were saying to women online. It can embolden people to be their worst self.' The anonymity the online interaction provides is taken by some as a dreadful freedom.

Did she get the sense that some men might think this kind of conversational opening was going to lead somewhere, or that it was more a form of trolling?

'I think for some of them they're annoyed by having had a bunch of conversations with women that didn't go where they wanted them to go, so they're just like, "is this going to happen or not?" For me, I wasn't looking for a lot, but I wanted them to indicate to me that they were reasonable human beings, you know?'

It can be hard to fathom what someone who takes this approach on dating apps is really expecting to happen. When I ask women what *they* think might be the reasoning behind the sending of nude pictures or overtly sexual messages (it's not something any of the straight men I talk to have experienced from women) in the opening exchanges with a stranger on a dating app, reasons proffered include: the exercise of power; a sense of frustration resulting from a high number of interactions which didn't lead to a date; that they genuinely think this is what women want because they would love to be sent nudes by a woman; or the fact that the internet has created a consequence-less space which allows people to act with impunity.

Dr Nicola Fox Hamilton has a PhD in cyberpsychology and is a lecturer in applied psychology and cyberpsychology in the Institute of Art, Design and Technology (IADT). Her research has focused on communication through technology, particularly in the areas of online dating, relationships and attraction. I put to her the reasons suggested by my interviewees, to see if they match with her findings.

'It is all of those things. A small percentage of men do it for power reasons. It's a malevolent reason to control somebody else's emotions, to make them feel fear, or shame, or disgust. That is probably most akin to offline flashing. Where it's not *really* about sex. They might get a sexual thrill out of it, but really it's more about power and control. That's about 10 per cent of the men who send dick pics, from the research. For the other 90 per cent, about half of them think that it's transactional: if they send the images, people will be excited by them, and send images in return. When you look at the research on gay men, they're more likely to send those, and get less upset by them. It's more acceptable within that community. But men don't seem to realise that women don't operate the same way.'

For a smaller but still substantial percentage, around 30 per cent, Dr Fox Hamilton says they get sexually excited by sending the pictures and think the woman on the receiving end will feel the same.

Research would suggest this is far from the case. 'Women feel disgusted, like their space is being invaded or violated, they *just* do not like them. And they cannot comprehend why men would send them.'

She refers to a rather grim piece of research conducted amongst adolescent men aged between seventeen and twenty. It was put to them that woman are overwhelmingly unhappy by receiving unsolicited sexual imagery, that it upsets them, and they don't like it.

'The guys' response was that women *have* to say that. That really women enjoy it, but if they say they enjoy it they'll be slut shamed. So they have to say that they're not. There's this bizarre understanding that there are double standards for women, and yet simultaneously, these men were not listening to women at all, but projecting their own beliefs on them. Because obviously they would *love* if women sent them nudes.'

My interviewees' sense that some men were lashing out because they were sick of not getting a response is also true.

'Men's primary difficulty with online dating is that they send loads of messages and they get very little response in return. It starts to make them feel like they're not attractive, nobody's interested in them. They often get quite anxious about it and start to create messages to just get some kind of reaction or response. It's also partly why sometimes, where women will say *I'm not interested* they'll write back and say *why aren't you interested?* Sometimes it's genuine; they really want to know what they can do better. They're not getting any feedback at all, and it makes it really difficult for them. But obviously that response is *not* an appropriate response to get a reaction out of women. It's not going to get them what they want.'

'I know men on their dating profiles will complain about women never wanting to meet up,' Betsy says. 'And I know that as a woman on a dating app you have more options. It's a buyers' market as a woman, right?' Betsy says with a smile. It's the first time I've heard this positive a spin from a woman on the abundance of men on online dating apps – more often the take on the wide choice available is that there are so many men but so few with any potential. A sense of having to wade through the dross, the very fact of abundance of choice only serving to highlight how few men there are who you might actually be interested in.

Betsy found her interactions with women to be of a completely different tone. Firstly, she found it easier to meet women through the apps, as opposed to IRL.

'Because you already know that a woman who's matching with you on a dating app is also queer, whereas I think as a woman – and I've talked about this with other queer women before – you're sort of hyper-aware of how men can be too aggressive in coming on to you. So women tend to be very cautious about not wanting to make each other feel uncomfortable. And the side effect of that is that you never know – a woman can be very direct with you and you're still like, oh she's just being nice. I don't really know. Which can lead to women just struggling to come on to each other.'

The dating apps, with their clear-cut box ticking apparatus, eradicate this potential opacity. 'If you're on the app, and you've matched with someone, you know they like you, or they're at least interested, so you can just have a talk.'

She went on more dates with men, in part simply because they were more plentiful. 'Also, as a bisexual woman, unfortunately I've had the experience, and talking to other bisexual women they've had it as well, of women who identify as lesbians sometimes not wanting to date you, because you also date men. I had that experience a couple of times with women I was talking to on dating apps here. When they found out that I had an ex-husband, or I was bisexual, they said they weren't interested anymore.'

The woman Betsy ended up going on a date with was also bisexual. 'I wouldn't want to speak to someone else's motivations but ... I guess I know for some women, lesbianism is really about centring women in their lives, and so they want to be with someone who also really centres women in their life. And I do respect that. But it can be a painful experience, to be rejected just for who you are, obviously.'

Betsy grew up in an Episcopalian family in New Hampshire. While her church itself was relatively moderate, her parents, especially her mother, were not. 'My mother had quite a fundamentalist mindset and was a lot more intense about Christianity than most of my community was.'

She never bothered to formally come out to her parents, knowing she would not have their support, and is now estranged from them. She assumes they know, as she has written about it on her blog, which she knows her mother reads, 'but in a very typical WASP family way, she just never brought it up.'

Queerness wasn't something she saw around her as a child. 'I grew up in a conservative Christian family. By the time I was thirteen, I remember my mother telling me that homosexuality was wrong, and I kind of knew that that wasn't correct.'

Luckily, she had a close group of good friends in high school, many of whom later 'turned out to be under the queer umbrella, although most of us didn't know it at the time, which is funny. But we talked about sexuality a lot'. Being an avid reader also gave her other perspectives.

She describes the imposter syndrome that she says can come with being bisexual. 'You don't have to be perfectly equal in your attractions to different genders to identify as bisexual, it just means that you're attracted to more than one gender. It takes a while, I know it did for me, to be able to say that you're bisexual, because you feel more attraction to one gender than another. Or you've had more experience with men or with women or whatever. But if you feel that attraction to more than one gender, you're allowed to call yourself bisexual,' Betsy smiles.

Sharon Nolan is a coordinator with Bi+ Ireland who lives in Galway. Originally from County Roscommon, she came out when she was seventeen. 'We would joke at events, "not feeling bi enough is the bi experience",' she laughs. 'We have nearly all felt like that at some point.'

Bi+ Ireland was founded in 2013. Previously, one of the only events that provided a specific bisexual space was a yearly USI LGBT+ conference called Pink Training. 'People would wait all year to go into a room with other bisexual people from across the country,' Sharon says. 'It would be almost a frantic space, because people would be like, "oh I want to talk about all the good things and all the bad things, and commiserate, and work together". And you're trying to do all that in a one-hour workshop.'

After the 2013 event, Aoife O'Riordan, a workshop facilitator, decided to create another space in which bisexual people could connect, so she set up a Facebook group, later asking people round the country to be co-ordinators for what became Bi+ Ireland.

The group now has about 1,500 members. 'When I joined, there were like eighty people in it, and I was so excited,' Sharon says. 'We used to do meet ups every second month. It was just having that specific space where you could go saying this is a bi space.'

Betsy quickly realised that what it came down to with online dating was, more than initial attractiveness, the other person's ability to hold a conversation.

'The people I had the most positive experiences with [weren't] necessarily the people that I found *most* physically attractive in their pictures. It was the people with whom it was easy to establish a back and forth. There are a lot of men who are just unable to hold a decent conversation. And I never came across that with any of the women I talked to.'

How do men react to her being bisexual?

'Positively, but not always in a good way,' she says, smiling and half rolling her eyes. 'I've never met a man who was disgusted by it or anything like that, but certainly you meet men who think that that means you're going to have a threesome or something. And that's not what it means. I mean, *maybe*, but that's not the point, you know,' she laughs. 'It can be fetishising. Or they want to hear you talk in great detail about your experiences.' Men's reaction to her bisexuality has become a litmus test for her in dating. Any man she has dated seriously understands that it is just a part of who she is.

There are unique challenges that come with being bisexual, in terms of finding belonging in both queer and non-queer communities, Betsy says. How do you express your queerness, stay in touch with it and not feel like you're repressing that, when you're in a monogamous – what Betsy describes as a 'straight-passing' – relationship? ('a relationship that looks straight to other people. It's not a straight relationship because I'm not straight'), I ask.

'I do hear queer people talk about how queerness is hypersexualised by straight people, that they think that the only way to express being gay is by having gay sex,' Betsy says. 'It's just part of who you are. So I think in a way, I would answer that in the same way that a straight person would.'

Her work is queer art, she writes queer stories. That is part of it. Another is her community: a lot of her friends are queer, quite a few of them are queer women in relationships with men. 'So we share that experience and are able to talk with each other about it.'

'Also I think, being queer and growing up, knowing that you have this part of you that isn't accepted by everyone, to various degrees affects your world view in ways I can't even articulate. My queerness is expressed in my world view no matter who I'm with.'

Sharon, who came out in rural Roscommon, notes that it does not really matter where you live – the important thing is to have a community of people that understands your experience.

'You could be surrounded by people, and know there's a thriving queer community there, but if you're the only queer person in your friend group or your family, that is to them unpaved territory. So there's a lot of weight, and a lot of burden that comes on someone. When I was living in a more rural area, I never felt like, this is so hard because

I'm bisexual, I was like, this is so hard because I'm alone. I don't know anyone who has this shared experience.'

Betsy was living in East Galway during the same-sex marriage referendum. She was out, she says, but it doesn't always come up in conversation. At the time she welcomed the chance to talk to people about the matter.

'Something that happened several times was that people in the pub or wherever would be having a conversation about gay marriage, and just very clearly assuming that everyone in the room was straight. And so I had the privilege of being able to out myself in that scenario, and watch people's perceptions change. Because they had maybe never met someone who said they were queer. And they already knew me and liked me. I wasn't just someone on the news, or something.'

Like Sharon, Betsy points to the importance of connecting with those who understand your experience from the inside out.

'I really appreciate dating other queer people, no matter what their gender is, because we have a profound experience in common. This sort of in-between experience. So there's a way in which dating a bisexual man, I would feel more in common with him than dating either a straight man or a lesbian. Because we have this shared sort of liminal experience.'

Quicker than she expected after she began dating, Betsy got into a relationship with a lovely man. It wasn't meant to happen, she laughs. James lives in Cork, neither wanted a long-distance relationship, but they matched while he was driving through Galway with his Bumble on, and they entered each other's radius.

'We were both kind of annoyed because we'd done long distance before, but we just really hit it off by text right away. I sent him a funny gif, and he sent one back that made me laugh, and we had like a gif war. It just turned out that we had a really similar sense of humour.'

He was nice, genuine, charming. Turns out it's much more effective than dick pics, she laughs, adding of the approach: 'it's sad that that's such a rare thing.'

James came to visit for a night, and Betsy brought her son to stay with his old childminder. This was something she had been doing for one weekend a month already. 'I really struggled with that at first, even before I had started dating. I felt a lot of guilt about needing time to myself. I adore my child, I love spending time with my child, but everybody needs time to themselves.'

Betsy and James would meet once a month, the first two times Betsy's son was with his childminder. After that, James and her son met and got on very well, so James would come and stay for the weekend, or Betsy and her boy would go to Cork.

'We were sort of a package deal the whole time,' she acknowledges. Having met him first when he was two and a half, her son has essentially known James, now his god-father, all his life.

Both recently out of long-term relationships, in getting together Betsy and James both figured that this was not going to be a forever after. But then the pandemic happened. Betsy's son's crèche was closed, and she was faced with several weeks (as we thought then) of having to work full time but also watch an active two-and-a-half-year-old.

She recalls how scary that felt. In a panic, she contacted James and asked him to help. He collected his laptop from work and immediately made his way to them from Cork.

He saved us, she smiles. But then they kind of saved him too, she adds, noting the unprepossessing situation of being a single man living in a city apartment throughout lockdown. She describes the difference of going into a marriage aged twenty-four, and a co-habiting arrangement in your thirties, both of you with one big relationship already under your belt.

'With my ex-husband, it was very passionate. It felt like this grand romance. We eloped together, and I had constructed this very compelling narrative in my head about it. Whereas with James it didn't feel like this swept-off-my-feet thing.'

Instead, they were very intentional, approaching it in a manner that was 'not starry-eyed at all. Because we were still planning on not ending up together afterwards. We were just in this situation.'

It wasn't just the pandemic. It was a practicality born out of experience. 'The fact that we're in our thirties, and also that I had been so burned by my previous relationship. We weren't so "oh we're meant to be together". We're just two people, we know the kinds of problems that can come up.' A weekly date night was put in place, but also a weekly night spent apart, each watching a movie on their own in a separate room in the house. There was a schedule for childminding, duties were apportioned out. 'Our ability to communicate was much better. I think that was thanks to what we had both learnt from our previous relationships.'

Betsy has that quality of a parent whose big relationship has ended. Never again will a romantic partner be at the absolute centre of their world – that relationship will never be the be-all and end-all.

'That's a self-confidence thing as well. I'm building a good life here, and if someone wants to be with me, they can make compromises for me. Because I think as women, we're always asking ourselves to make sacrifices.'

Betsy has realised that while she first moved to Carraroe for financial reasons, she now chooses to stay there.

'I went into dating not wanting a relationship. I really found that I *liked* being a single parent. I wasn't looking to fill a gap or anything like that. I wanted to go on dates, I wanted to have sex, I wanted to restore that part of my life a little bit. But what I really wanted, the driving force of my life that has brought me here, was finding steady ground for myself and my kid. That I would be building something safe for my life that would be centred around myself and my child, rather than something I'd have to compromise on with someone else. And that's something I still really believe in. And that I think a lot of women don't realise they're giving up, when they enter into committed relationships.'

'I'm genuinely happy being single. And I think there's this *incredibly* pervasive narrative that you need a partner to be happy.'

It's not that she is closed off forever from the concept of having a partner. And more specifically, it is not that her and James might not get back together. But it is not the only, or indeed the main, goal.

'Why are we telling women that the key to your happiness is a heterosexual marriage? It's ridiculous. That's not to say that it can't be a beautiful, valuable thing, but it's not, like, the solution to your problems.'

The solution to Betsy's problems was much more tangible than a relationship. Before I leave, Betsy brings me on a tour of her home. Once all one big space, the building has now been divided into a number of small rooms that lie beyond the large kitchen with its high ceilings. Downstairs there is a small workspace for Betsy, her five book covers framed on the wall, her child's room, teddies overflowing from the bed to the floor, her own room, a large bathroom and a spare room.

Before Betsy found the Old Knitting Factory, she had already begun to harbour an idea of founding a free, creative retreat for single mothers, with childcare included. 'I never anticipated being a single parent, but I'm really proud of the fact that I hang it together. And I *love* other single mothers. That's why I wanted to make this space.'

She also wanted to create that permanent home for her and her son. The place where she now lived, with its peaceful surroundings and extra bedroom, would be perfectly suited to such a venture. She was renting, but when she approached her landlord, he agreed to allow her to purchase.

The asking price was entirely beyond what she would be able to raise herself, and she was turned down by the banks for a mortgage. Undaunted, Betsy crowdfunded and raised almost half the money needed.

By the eve of the deadline for the full amount, however, in the November before we meet, Betsy was still 50 per cent short of the amount required. By this stage, she says, she had gone through the extreme stress stage and out the other side, coming to terms with this not working out. And then a friend rang. Her mother wanted to make a donation. Betsy was to call her. She did, thinking the woman wanted to give a small amount as so many other people generously had.

'How much do you need?' her friend's mother asked. Betsy told her the outstanding amount. The woman was a philanthropist and gave Betsy the money she needed to buy the Old Knitting Factory, where she will live with her son and create a retreat for other mothers.

'It was like a total fairy-tale ending,' she smiles. 'If it was one of my novels, I wouldn't have ended it like that, 'cause it's too nice.'

Betsy had found her home.

Part Three
Finding Your Tribe

12

You're Usually Not My Type

Sandrine's boyfriend Tony first stood out because he didn't call her hot. 'He called me beautiful,' she smiles. Until then it had always felt as if she had been overly sexualised by guys: 'Oh you're so hot, I can't wait until my friends know about this.' Or they might want to keep the relationship a secret: 'Oh, it's an exciting thing, but let's not tell anyone.' Or, 'We're going out, but let's not put an official name to it.'

All of this meant that when, after three weeks of dating each other, Tony called Sandrine his girlfriend it nearly gave her a heart attack, she smiles now. Previously, she had been with people and that status had never been given to the relationship. 'It was always something that was at the back of my mind. Was it a sense of embarrassment? Or "I don't want to be labelled an interracial couple and have to deal with the intense conversations about race and racism that we would need to have?"'

He calls her hot *now*, she smiles quizzically. They've been going out for a little bit over three years, having met in Limerick, where she is studying for a PhD. 'But at that time when I didn't trust guys, he just really saw me as *me*, as opposed to this fetishised version of a Black girl. Literally that one word, beautiful, was what made a difference. 'Okay, I'll go on a date with you. Because I thought he's not like the rest.'

Sandrine grew up in County Carlow, where dating as a teenager had always felt isolating. All her friends began having boyfriends around the age of sixteen. 'I'd always be the single friend, going along with it. I remember I had a crush on this one boy. At that age you think, this is the love of my life. But I remember him saying "oh my kind of girl is someone who's tanned and blonde and stuff". Straight away I was out of the picture.'

This happened a lot, she says. Guys friend-zoning her. 'Because they had a perception of the girlfriend that they wanted to have at that age. Social media wasn't as big then, but from magazines the standard of beauty was always the blonde, Western beauty standard. I was conditioned from such a young age.'

She grew up wondering if she should, 'try to not be attracted to white boys. Should I try to be attracted to Black guys? But when I *would* find a Black guy attractive when I was younger, they might say "no, I want a white girlfriend". From such a young age I was hyper-aware of who I was attracted to. When I was attracted to white guys there was this sort of resistance where they always made it abundantly clear that blonde was their type. When I was attracted to Black guys, they also made it clear that blonde was their type. So I was constantly stuck in a limbo of where I thought that I was just not desirable.'

It made her self-conscious. If someone professed to like her she would feel unsure whether she could trust what they said. 'Do they like me for me, or is this kind of – as horrible as it sounds – an experiment? Are they going through a phase?'

'I like you, but I don't think I'll act on that.'

'You're usually not my type.'

'You're pretty for a Black girl.'

When she thought about wanting to have children in the future, she felt that she would most likely do IVF because, 'I just could not imagine being with someone. That's the perception I'd gotten. "Unless you look like this, then I don't want it." Or if they did want me, then it was kind of for that trophy element.'

'Going to discos in third and fourth year, I would go in thinking, well no one is going to find me attractive. So there was a very lonely element. I never really thought much about it until I moved to Limerick, and really found my place and my sense of identity – nothing to do with my parents, or how I was brought up, but how much of a lonely childhood I would have had.'

As she got older, in going on a date she would feel anxious about a man's intentions. Was this a novelty for him? 'Had they told their friends that they're going on a date with a Black girl? I couldn't really go there with the initial butterflies, because I just did not know what to expect.'

Her friends who were white had boyfriends. It became an equation in her head. 'To be Black is to be ugly and single. Those things really stuck with me even when I first went to college and started getting my confidence. I did not trust guys at all around that kind of thing.'

She had moved to County Carlow with her family in 2006, when she was eleven, going into fourth class. Sandrine was born in a refugee camp in Tanzania in 1995 and lived there for two years with her parents. When she was around two they moved to Rwanda, where her sister was born in 1999. They then moved to Kenya and lived there until 2006.

The year the family came to Ireland was the year Trócaire established a fundraising box for Rwanda. 'Anytime you would say you where you were from, that was what it was about. I just remember going through that moment, hating being from there, because it was that stereotype of what Africa was.'

It was a shock to those around her that she spoke English – along with Swahili it was one of her first languages, something she would have to repeatedly explain. On entering her new school Sandrine was made to do extra classes, usually aimed at foreign students.

'I aced that,' she says dryly, explaining that it felt as if she had had to prove herself. There were three other African children in her class. 'I was Rwandese, and they were Nigerian, but people were very quick to push us together because we were the foreign kids.'

She recalls a conversation years later with a friend, who told her she used to worry about Sandrine through primary and secondary school. 'Because I'd always gravitate towards white friends, never Black friends. She would worry about that, that I was kind of placing myself in that othering. She wondered did I not want to be friends with other African people, to kind of share that.'

Sandrine explained that her parents had brought her and her siblings up to think, 'your friends are the people that you are friends with. It shouldn't be about colour, and there shouldn't be this sense of, okay so you experienced racism, or you experienced othering, so let's bond over that.'

She recalls being told 'you're acting white' or 'you're very Europeanised'.

Sandrine now has two younger brothers as well as her sister. The family lived in the town centre, in a housing estate.

'It felt very small,' she says of growing up in Carlow. 'When it came to college, I wanted to get as far away as possible. It was a sense of you knew everyone, and everyone knew everyone's business, and coming from our family, we were a Black family, we were Rwandese, and there weren't any other Rwandese there. We were very hyper-aware.'

On a school trip to the University of Limerick, she realised it would take three trains to get there from her hometown. No one will know who I am, she thought. Perfect.

'It was just much easier to reconstruct what I thought it meant to be Irish, and what I thought it meant to be Black,' she explains of moving to Limerick as a student. 'In Carlow it was very pressuring,' she says, describing some of the assumptions she dealt with. 'If you weren't Nigerian, and you were Rwandese, you might hear, well my Nigerian friend is allowed to do this, so do you do that?'

People also made assumptions about her relationship with her parents, and how strict they might be.

'They raised us very liberally, and to be very free-minded. I think that confused other kids as well. It was considered weird that my parents allowed me to do arts subjects in college and allowed me to do creative things. There wasn't that pressure of, oh you're a migrant, become a doctor, or do business.'

Sandrine is twenty-six now and describes herself as being unapologetically Black. But certain situations will still send her back to her younger self.

'I love my Blackness and my African hair, everything like that, but if I'm the only Black person in a room I can still crumple back into my sixteen-year-old self.' It's something she has tried really hard to overcome.

'If I walk into a nightclub and I'm holding my boyfriend's hand and there are stares, I'll wonder, do they think he's with me for sex or what do they think he's doing with a Black girl?'

Men will approach Tony in a nightclub to comment on their relationship: 'She must be so crazy in bed' or 'Your sex life must be unreal. You're so lucky.' Of the many ways in which this is offensive, Sandrine feels put in the position of trophy wife. 'They would comment on my appearance, always in a very sexual nature, which goes back to the fetishisation of Black women.'

He has a picture of her on his screensaver. 'If he shows people, they sometimes say to him "oh fair play to you". Within the interracial relationship that we have, I'm always very aware of that oversexualisation which is projected onto me.'

Together they have had to figure out how to navigate these kinds of situations. Tony would get upset, but Sandrine hated when people spoke on her behalf.

'It's a defence mechanism I have, so he'd have to stand there and not say anything because we would have a fight if he did. I would say, "I could have stood up for myself."'

It creates a consciousness within her of the burden placed on her boyfriend. It has taken a long time to not take this on as something that is in some way her responsibility. Previously, when racist incidents occurred, Sandrine felt as though her former boyfriends were annoyed with her – as though she was the one who caused the hassle

'In our first year in UL, if we were walking together holding hands, people would always stare. I've gone through that, I just didn't want him to go through it. I don't like a big spectacle made of it, but I can always tell when someone is about to say something rude, I can just see it in their mannerism. But he's never experienced that. So I got to the point where I wouldn't hold his hand in public, but that would cause us problems, because he'd think I was embarrassed, as opposed to me just trying to protect him.'

Tony, who is twenty-seven, was adopted from Romania by an Irish family when he was two. 'We connect on that level, on our first date we talked about that. When I told him I was a refugee, he didn't react the way people usually do, you know, feeling sorry for me, how have you come this far?'

Instead his attitude was more, oh, so we both had a late start in life.

Now, she's happy for Tony to speak out more if something arises. He will pull people aside, say that upset my girlfriend, it made me uncomfortable. It's not embarrassing, he tells Sandrine, it should not be happening to you.

'In the past, it would have been a very uncomfortable situation, and I would have thought if this is always going to happen, maybe I should just date Black. But you can't really force yourself into dating someone who looks like you just so you don't experience these things in life.'

Ejiro Ogbevoen is a counsellor and psychotherapist and founder of Black Therapists Ireland, an organisation which offers the opportunity of work with Black therapists living in Ireland, which she created because she felt that, 'there are certain things in which a white therapist just cannot hold the space for a person of colour. Just because your experiences do not match. That doesn't mean that good work cannot be done [with a white therapist], but we have experienced racism, discrimination, we get it in a way that probably a white person wouldn't.'

She gives her observations on what people in interracial relationships might be dealing with.

'People feel it's all nice and dandy, that we understand it's a diverse world, but just don't cross the line,' she says. 'And being in an interracial relationship is crossing the line. It's so visual, and people don't like that, both people of colour and white people. And if it's a Black man with a white woman, you're a sell-out. Look at us, we're trying to raise the Black community, we're trying to do this work, and you go off and you marry a white woman. Quit messing with the boundaries.

'A lot of white people think this shouldn't be happening: "I know we're all free and safe and able to do whatever we want, but I want you to know, this doesn't look good. I don't like it, and I will let you know."'

The turning point for Sandrine and Tony came during a trip to Dublin to see Post Malone. 'We were in an elevator, and there were two white girls, I don't know if they were drunk or something. We were holding hands, it was Valentine's Day. They looked me up and down and one of them said, "God, I love being white." In an elevator – we couldn't leave. I didn't know what to say, and Tony just lost it.'

That's when she knew that rather than trying to always fight her battles herself, feeling constantly on high alert but trying to hide that from Tony, it was something they would deal with together.

It's the sense of always being aware, Sandrine says. 'Hypervigilance is that state of constant awareness of the threats that are around you,' explains Ejiro. 'And the possible threats that might come your way. It's connected to that survival instinct that we all have, where you find yourself in that fight-or-flight mode. It is human nature, but it is something that, in our environment, should be temporary. If you get to that state of fight or flight, and you cannot switch off, that is when your environment becomes almost in itself a threat.'

It has taken a really long time, Sandrine says, but she has found her community and come to terms with the idea that there are different ways of being Irish. 'Our friends group is so diverse. I've found my people there. If anything happens, we're all able to stand up for each other.

'I don't have to apologise anymore. That was something of which I was very aware, of being the only Black friend in a friend group, where if something racist was to happen I'd be the one apologising for making everyone feel uncomfortable, even though it was happening to me. Now I don't even have to say anything. My friends and Tony, they stand up for me straight away.'

Would she bring kids up in a small town, I ask? 'No, I absolutely wouldn't. I'd have to be somewhere diverse.' She cannot escape the hyperawareness, it's not something she wants instilled in her own children.

'When I look at little kids being able to have such diverse friends, I'm so envious of that, because we didn't have that. I would have to raise my kids in a multicultural setting, where they just wouldn't feel that sense of closedness, and also of being the only Black or mixed-race person here. It was just too traumatic for me growing up, so I just wouldn't want that to happen.'

'Being in a place where no one else looks like you. There's that sense of hyperawareness, where you feel very, very different.' As much as she could, she would protect them from feeling 'otherised. And I think small places, small communities, which aren't as diverse, *really* do that. I just wouldn't want that cycle to repeat itself'.

13

Small-Town Life Wasn't for Me

From a young age, Deirdre was aware that she was trans, she just didn't have the right word for it. 'My earliest memories are that I knew.' Growing up in a small one-street village in the midlands in 1980s Catholic Ireland, it 'certainly wasn't something that you talked about. Even at a very young age, I knew it wasn't something that was acceptable'.

Deirdre, who is now fifty-three, was the eldest of five. Her mother ran the home, her father was a factory worker. Their cousins lived next door and the two houses shared a back yard, and as children they played together as a gang.

'It's just a small one-street village; it was on the main road but when they built the motorway it was bypassed. Since the boom, lots more housing estates were built, so the fields at the back of our house where we would play as kids are now full of houses. You don't know you don't have much money. We were fed and we were loved and looked after. When they could afford things, we would get things.' They went on holidays, she adds with a smile. 'One year we went to Bettystown and stayed in a tent for a week. But one year we went to Galway and stayed in a B&B.'

Deirdre remained living at home throughout college and for several years afterwards, working locally but not moving from her parents' house until sometime in her mid- to late twenties. She moved abroad, then came home and bought her own house, also in the midlands. She got married and, after their separation, moved to the apartment where she now lives, in an 'even more remote spot' in the county, where 'nobody knows her'.

'I was a late bloomer,' she says with a smile. 'And there was guilt there as well. Because I was very close to my mother for years. I remember once telling her I was going to look for an apartment and she was very upset, so that kind of put the kibosh on that for a while.'

One of her earliest memories is of playing with some old clothes of her mother's in the 'good' wardrobe, 'one of those old-fashioned ones that had a mirror on the door, a little key, a big old heavy sort of Narnia thing.'

She had found a skirt and was trying it on. 'It just felt natural to me. I didn't think about why I wanted to do this, didn't analyse it, I just did it, it felt right.'

Her mother caught her that day and later made a joke about it at the dinner table. 'I don't think she meant any- thing by it, but I was embarrassed.' It didn't stop Deirdre trying on clothes – 'a lot of my childhood was spent trying on clothes whenever I could' – but she knew from then that this was something no one could know about. 'I think that was when I realised, this isn't the done thing. That's when

I sort of knew to keep it quiet. And from then I was very much in the closet for a lot of my life, until I eventually came out.'

She speaks gently, occasionally fiddling with the dark hair that floats about her shoulders. As part of the process of coming out, she went to elocution lessons, she tells me, as we sit under a wisteria-clad pergola, an unlikely beauty spot in the grounds of a hospital Deirdre is attending.

Growing up, she never felt part of the community. 'I was always apart in a way. I don't mean that to sound snobby or anything, I just felt that way. The small-town life wasn't for me, sort of thing. Loads of people I know who grew up there still live in the village and are in and out of their mother's houses every day. That just never appealed to me. Even though it took me a while to move away,' she says with a laugh. 'It was just never something I wanted. Because I don't want people knowing my business. Everybody knows everybody.'

She describes her teenage years with a sense of bleakness: the smallness of the world, the dearth of anyone who might be going through something similar.

'When you're growing up in a small rural village in Ireland, it's a very enclosed space, and it's very, very claustrophobic. I was sent to a Christian Brothers school. We weren't taught about sexuality, we weren't even taught about periods for girls. When I think about it ...' she says wryly.

For teenagers, there was little in the way of entertainment. 'It felt very enclosed. There's nowhere to go. There was a local community centre, and you could go there and hang out. Basically just a hall. Torture for somebody like me. I felt like I didn't fit in, I felt awkward around girls, and around other people.'

There was a snooker club, with three full-size snooker tables, Deirdre adds, but it was called The Boys Club. 'That might be a lie that only boys were allowed join, but only boys did.'

As a teenager, Deirdre attended an all-boys school. 'I was attracted to girls and, I'll be honest, I was relieved. Because of the oppressive attitudes of the time, I didn't want to be gay, so I was glad I wasn't gay.'

She had her first 'sort of serious girlfriend' in secondary school, around the age of fifteen, a girl she met on the school bus. They went out for about a year and 'of course she broke my heart', she laughs. 'You know, your first serious heartbreak at that age, it's all par for the course. I was absolutely besotted and infatuated. That first romance, where everything is heady and wonderful. It was quite something.'

She was relieved she was attracted to girls, she adds, because, 'I sort of thought well maybe this will help me overcome this other side of me that I want to repress and keep hidden, that I don't want to let out. But it didn't. It didn't stop me cross-dressing, it didn't stop me wanting to be someone else. But I kept fighting and fighting and fighting. Because I did not want to have to be that person. I did not want to have to go through that.'

Deirdre talked to nobody about any of this. 'It was probably my deepest – I don't want to say darkest – secret, because it's obviously not a dark thing, but at the time, that's what it felt like. It felt like a deep, dark secret, and there was absolutely no way I could tell anybody.' She experienced huge shame and guilt, she recalls. Being known, the absolute lack of anonymity in her community, made it harder to then change, to be the person who is going to be different. 'Because it's such a small community, everyone knows who you are. That makes it more difficult to change and to stand out.'

Throughout her teenage years she was caught crossdressing a couple of times. Women's clothes were found in her bedroom. 'My father asked me at some stage was I some sort of pervert. It's hard to get over something like that. We're still ... I wouldn't say at loggerheads,' she says, hesitating, 'but we're still awkward around each other.'

Being a teenager is hard to begin with. Being a trans teenager is harder, she says. 'It was so difficult ... I wouldn't wish it on anybody.' She describes dressing in women's clothes as stolen moments. 'Moments here and there where you could just, even if it was only for twenty minutes, you could be yourself. Just the stress of having to come down from that and come back to my dull mundane life. Looking back, I honestly don't know how I got through it. But you do. You get through it because you have to. When I look back now I go, Jesus Christ, how did I get through that without something terrible happening to me, or without doing something terrible to myself?'

It was through the internet that she first heard the word transgender. Visibility, while growing up in 1980s Ireland was, unsurprisingly, a problem. There were no trans people in her world whom she could aspire to be. Deirdre describes the bargaining process she would engage in with herself, the effort for self-acceptance stymied by growing up in a place steeped in societal prejudice. 'The very few trans people you might see on screen were either made fun of, or they were serial killers, or victims of serial killers in movies. So I would think, well at least I'm not a trans-sexual. I just thought I was somebody who likes wearing women's clothes. Like a hobby. This is how I validated it with myself. First of all it was, at least I'm not gay, then it was at least I'm not a transsexual. Which was the term in those days. It was always sort of, okay, I can accept *this*, if I'm not *that*. Because that's the sort of environment that I grew up in, that's the Ireland I grew up in.'

She was an altar boy for a number of years. 'My father would have been quite strict religiously. We went to mass every Sunday. You would say the rosary at home some-times. He wasn't an authoritarian as such, but he was quite religious himself, and that sort of filtered down to the rest of the family.'

Faced with all of this, it took her a long time to accept that she was transgender.

'I think it was more the prejudices around me, and within my own home. A big part of me always wanted to please my father, and to be a man: to do the socially acceptable thing as the eldest son, so for a long time that was why I sort of denied who I was. And the fact that there were no visible trans women … I thought I was the only person that felt like this. There was nobody I felt I could talk to about it.'

As an adult in her twenties, all her sexual encounters bar one were in the context of serious relationships: 'it was never casual'. She was shy, an introvert, and 'this is probably going to sound very naive, but at the time we had the AIDS crisis, and that was being drummed into us', she recalls.

'At those moments, I always thought, I'm a man, and … I hate to say I'm doing manly things – but this means that I'm normal as such. Or as normal as can be. If I look back at it, and I think about it pretty hard, definitely, I would have preferred to be the woman in those encounters. It's a strange way of saying it I suppose, it's hard to vocalise, but I suppose the more submissive partner might be a better way of putting it.'

Deirdre never talked to any of the women she dated about how she was feeling until she met the woman she would go on to marry, whom she told she was cross-dressing. 'I told her before we were married, and she was extremely upset about it, and that made me feel hugely, *hugely* guilty.

'Guilt because I had made her so upset. Shame because this was a part of me that I was already thoroughly ashamed of. I had been open and vulnerable enough to share it with somebody and I didn't get the reaction … I don't know what reaction I was expecting, but I certainly didn't get the reaction I wanted. It made it even worse. It made me push it back even further.'

Deirdre said she 'wouldn't cross-dress anymore. Again, I would repress everything. I pushed everything down and hid everything. For quite a number of years of our marriage I didn't cross-dress.'

They were relatively happy, she says now. They had several children. Eventually, however, it was clear that things were not right in the marriage. 'I always say it wasn't this gender issue that pushed us apart, we were having rows anyway, not getting along.' Separating made her realise she needed to change things drastically. 'We're only on this planet for a short time, and I needed to be myself. I didn't want to go on pretending anymore. I think that was the thing that eventually pushed me over the line to just accept that this is who I was.'

She had been very good at hiding 'that part of me. I was a very regular guy I suppose. A little bit shy and awkward at times, and I didn't like sport', she adds with a laugh. 'But in all other ways I was fairly regular. It can't have been good for my mental health. But the world accepted the face I turned towards it.'

Looking back, she can see it did huge damage to who she was as a person, and to her integrity. Having said that, she says, 'coming from all those trials, all those issues that I faced, that is why I am who I am today. And it's why I am the stronger person I am today. Because of all those experiences that I had.'

There was great solace after her marriage ended. Living on her own, she again began dressing as she wanted. 'And going out in public as Deirdre. It was such a huge relief to be able to express that part of me. To be able to just be me. And realise that it wasn't just cross-dressing, it was that this was who I was. Who I was inside. I really needed to be true to myself. That's when I started on the path to transition.'

She was in her mid-forties at the time. 'If I'm lucky I probably have another forty or forty-five years left on this planet. I've already spent half my life trying to please other people, trying to be the person other people thought I should be. I just didn't want to do that anymore. I couldn't do it anymore.' She has remained living in the midlands.

She was never that into the trans scene in Dublin, she says, because she lives too far away. There was a club off Liffey Street called Amanda Barry's, however, that she would visit occasionally. 'You could go there and change, you could bring clothes with you. They had a bar and a television. For me, I could go there, change into my clothes and then head out and go to the cinema, just do ordinary things, walk 'round the shops, go into a bookshop. That's all I ever wanted to do as Deirdre. And to be seen as a woman.' She has never wanted to live in Dublin, but it is easier to be her true self there. The anonymity suits her.

'So much easier. Nobody knew you. There was no fear of being recognised.' At the beginning, there is always that fear that someone will recognise you. 'That someone's going to go "look, that's a man". But also that somebody would recognise you. Eventually I got the courage to go out more and more in my local town as myself. But initially there was that huge fear. That's going to be amplified in a smaller community.'

Going home for the first time as Deirdre, to the house where she grew up and her parents still lived, was terrifying. 'I sat in the car for ages before plucking up the courage to ring the doorbell.' Now, any potential reactions from the wider community do not bother her, but initially she was petrified. Hyper-aware of everyone who walked towards her, she found herself, 'watching them for reactions ... there's possibly danger, but there's also the possibility they might read you. Might say "oh that's a man in a dress". They might make fun of you. Might attack you. So you're constantly aware. You've all this adrenaline flowing through you as well. Because of that, it's super exciting and super terrifying. It takes a long time to get over that, and just to be at ease with yourself.'

The bravest thing a trans person can do is step outside their own front door, Deirdre reflects. Initially she would map her route in her head before leaving the house: where were the safe places; where not to go; where might have public toilets that would be safe to use. She only went out in broad daylight, because it seemed safer to be out when there were lots of other people around.

'It's easier to hide a tree in the forest rather than go out in the middle of the night. Although I know a lot of trans people who, when they go out, go out in the middle of the night. There were a lot of excursions before I became really comfortable with who I was. With my expression of my gender, I suppose.'

She bought a book, *How to Be a Woman Though Male*, by Virginia Charles Prince. It covered things like how women hold a cigarette, how to sit, deportment. 'For a long time, I studied and studied that book. When you sit, you sit with your knees together. And then when you're out in public, you're supposed to be remembering all these things. The way you walk, the way you have to hold yourself.' She sighs. It was exhausting.

Eventually, she thought, fuck it, I don't care if people realise I'm trans. 'When that moment clicked in my brain – once I stopped caring about what people think – anytime I went out in public there was never an issue because I was comfortable in my own skin. And people didn't look twice at me. I don't know if I passed, and I don't care if I did. It's when I stopped caring whether I passed or not that I stopped getting hassle on streets.' This took years, she adds.

There is a difference between coming out to the world at large and the specific individuals in your life. 'That's always a tricky one. It's always a difficult process. Do you tell people face to face?' Her sister was lovely, accepting and supportive. Other family members were not, and remain so. 'I've told lots of people in lots of different ways. Reactions have gone from stunned silence, to okay, let's not talk about this again, to acceptance, to that's wonderful.'

She came out to her mother directly, who told Deirdre's father. It would be years before her parents spoke to her again. 'We would have seen each other at family events like the blessing of the graves, and my granny's anniversary mass. I would have always gone to those things,' she says of her siblings. 'And there were always sandwiches and tea back at my mum's house. It was tradition. Once I came out, I stopped getting invited to all those things.'

Then: 'I got a call from my mother to tell me she was dying – that was the first contact I had had from her in over four years.'

Deirdre's mother died in January 2021. 'I went to the funeral. It was difficult because obviously, in a small village like where I'm from, everybody knows everybody. It was my first time seeing relatives and people from home who knew me before I transitioned. To have to do that at a funeral was very, very difficult. I was cold-shouldered by some but not others. It was a difficult time, people were grieving.'

She describes little moments of happiness that sometimes come out of the blue. The first day she took hormones, the 'huge sense of relief, I was finally here'. When someone treats you 'as the person you are presenting as'. Swimming, at first one of the most difficult things she did since she transitioned. It took her a long time to build up the courage. 'Because I'm just not comfortable putting my body out there, and putting on a swimsuit doesn't leave a lot to the imagination.' Now it's one of the most rewarding things she can do for herself mentally. She loves swimming in the sea, feels entirely relaxed and at home. 'I don't feel burdened by my body, the water has taken all of that burden away from me, it's just holding me there, and it feels so comfortable. It's sort of like a blanket around me. I think it's the only time where that alarm bell isn't ringing in my head, when I'm just floating in the water. It really is my safe space.'

I wonder if she has found a sense of community in her adult life, beyond the one she grew up in but never felt quite part of. She smiles and says, 'I'm going to say yes and no. You sort of find your tribe; I have found a coterie of really close friends. Most of them are cis women, living in Dublin. It seems weird saying it, but I don't have any close trans friends. People think there's a trans cabal running things. There's not. We're a very diverse and scattered bunch of people.'

Deirdre's marriage separation was about six years ago, and she has not been in a relationship since.

'My transition has taken up a huge chunk of my time and energy, and then lockdown happened. So it hasn't really been an issue for me. I've been just focusing on my healthcare.' She's okay with that. 'I'm not pining to meet somebody. I love being on my own, to be honest, it's much less complicated.'

A year ago, if you had asked her about the possibility of a relationship, she would have said she wasn't interested. 'But now I'm not dismissing the possibility.'

She would be open about everything from the get-go, Deirdre smiles. Nothing would persuade her to ever go back to not being fully honest about who she is. 'I'm not going into that state again where I'm hiding part of who I am from people. You accept me for who I am, or you don't, and that's just it.'

Whoever she was dating would know she is transgender, 'and that is it', she says firmly. 'If you can't accept that that's who I am, then I'm not interested. I'm not going to go back. I am who I am, and you can like it or leave it at this stage.'

14

I Didn't Want to Be Alone

When she was considering ending her marriage, Emma worried that she would never meet anyone new. 'What if I'm still here at fifty, sixty, seventy with nobody, because I have children – who's going to want to date a 32-year-old with kids?' A mother of two boys, now thirteen and seven, Emma is from a small village in the north-west.

She lives in a large town in the same area where she works full time as a nurse. Her marriage ended eight years ago, and she moved because she needed better childcare options.

Now aged thirty-nine, after she and her husband separated she began dating almost immediately. 'I am, like, the *queen* of dating,' Emma says with relish, and a huge smile. She's very pretty, bubbly and light-spirted. Even when she's telling me the harder parts of her story, she often laughs and rolls her eyes as if she finds the whole thing amusing.

'I love it,' she admits of dating. 'I think you meet the most weird and wonderful people, and you get to know who you are.'

For her, dating in the aftermath of a break-up was an antidote to the demolition of one's esteem, and a way of telling herself that she was not alone, that others had gone through the same thing. It also provided some semblance of hope that there would be a future, at a time when it can feel like your life is closing down.

'I know all of that sounds very American,' she says. 'But I honestly think when your marriage breaks up, you lose your confidence, you're in a bad place, really you need to just get yourself out there and realise you're still attractive. That other people have gone through similar crap. That just because you have children doesn't mean that you're never going to meet somebody again. Because these are the things that you think when you separate.'

There were aspects of her position that were freeing: she didn't *need* anything from a prospective partner. 'I didn't need a daddy. And I didn't need a mortgage. I have my own money, I'm on a decent income. I suppose I was looking to date somebody because I enjoyed their company. I just wanted to date somebody for the relationship, for fun and sex.'

Meeting someone in real life didn't seem like a possibility – in fact any of the dates Emma has been on were with men she met online – so she immediately signed up to Tinder and Plenty of Fish. A friend in work had separated around the same time and in quiet moments during a shift

173

they would pore over their phones, scrolling the apps. 'We would sit there on night duty and go through them.'

The attention she received was unbelievable, she recalls with a laugh. 'Everybody liked my profile. I couldn't believe it.' It took her a year or so of online dating to realise that men swiped right with an abandon missing from her and her friend's 'fine-tooth comb' approach. 'They like all the profiles, and then they have hope that some of them will like them back.'

On an early date a man told her, 'If it has a pulse I swipe right. He was like, "You must know this? It doesn't matter what they look like, because even if they're not attractive, if they seem like an easy lay, or whatever, we'll go down that road. And maybe they'll become a friend."'

Unsurprisingly, this date went nowhere. 'I was raging. But inside I was like, this is why when as women we hit a profile that we like, they always match. Women are fussier. We'll take our time, we might go through the profile, we'll look at a few of the pictures before we like it. They just go yes, yes, yes, yes, yes, yes. And then whatever comes back comes back.'

Although she was thirty-three when she began dating, in the aftermath of her marriage ending, she set her age range to early forties, sometimes slightly older.

'You never go for the guy in his mid-thirties, the stud with the six pack. Because you know they're going to have a string of women after them. Life's not worth that.' Emma was looking for 'an older man who's done that, sowed their oats, wants to settle down. Because when I was dating I always wanted it to be a relationship. I never wanted it to be a one-night stand, a two-night stand, a three-week thing, I always wanted to take it slowly, see how I got on with the person.'

The first few encounters were interesting, she laughs. She was unaware that there was an expectation amongst the men she was talking to on Tinder that they would sleep together on the first date. She was surprised, because their interactions hadn't suggested the disposability of a one-off interaction, she explains. The kind of conversations they were having, the exchange of numbers, the following each other on Instagram, would suggest a potential bedding in of some sorts, if the date went well. Or so Emma thought.

'I assumed that that meant we're meeting for a drink, for a conversation. I didn't realise that they thought, we're going to have sex tonight,' she recalls. 'A lot of men will say to you, "But isn't Tinder just for the ride?" I assumed when people said that they meant the 23-year-old on Tinder. I didn't think they meant the mature adults with families and children.' As such, the first few dates were 'an absolute disaster, where I would have realised very quickly, your man thinks that we're actually going back to his house tonight'.

There was a date with a man in a hotel somewhere between where they both lived. When she arrived, he was on his second drink. Emma, driving, ordered a soda water and lime. 'I didn't think much about it. I thought maybe he had a friend he was going to stay with. We're sitting there and he's talking about his life. This is what I didn't understand. He was telling me about his dad who had died, he was telling me about his dog. Very much disclosing very personal stuff. Then he was on pint number three, and he said, "Are you not having a drink?" I was like, "Sure I'm driving."'

'Driving?' her companion replied. 'Sure, aren't you staying here with me tonight?'

'Straight out. I was like, "No. What gave you the impression that I was staying here tonight? I've a babysitter in my house minding my children. I'm on a time limit here, man." He had a night set up for himself, and thought I was rowing in. And he was *shocked.*'

He was a very good-looking man, the most handsome she has ever been on a date with, and she wonders whether that might have affected his expectations. 'He had a lot going for him. He was a rugby player, he had a good job, he had a house.'

She has had one-night stands but doesn't like them. 'I can't cope, because l always feel like it's a rejection. I become emotionally involved too quickly if I sleep with someone.'

Looking back, she can see that with many of the men she was going for there were obvious red flags, which she ignored: too much drinking, the relationship being based around socialisation, being sexually incompatible, lack of prioritising the relationship.

'Now I look at him and think, My god, what did I ever see in you?' she says of one man. 'I just clearly wanted a partner/ boyfriend/companion. I didn't want to be alone at that stage of my life. Some women are like that. They struggle being single, being the one on couples' nights out or at weddings alone. As if it somehow reflected on me. Was I too fussy, or should I just settle for what I could get? That is who I am. I wanted somebody there. I keep my social circle really small. And if I wanted to go to the cinema, I'd want it to be with a man. I didn't want it to be with my friends. I didn't want to go to dinner with my girlfriends, I wanted to be wined and dined by a man, this kind of crap.'

Growing up, Emma never had a relationship until after school when at seventeen she met her husband. 'My dad was really strict. I wasn't allowed have a boyfriend, I wasn't allowed go to discos, I wasn't allowed to wear skirts. I know that sounds really, really ridiculous, but I wasn't allowed to wear skirts. My mother always had myself and my sister in jeans. And I knew as I got a little bit older that it was my dad who was insisting on that.'

As a teenager, she would read at mass every Saturday evening in the small village where she grew up. 'I was a real Holy Joe,' she says with a smile.

One summer evening she met one of her friends from school afterwards and they lingered, chatting. At one point, Emma's father drove by. The following Saturday, as she left for mass, he told his daughter, 'You be straight home after mass, you're not to be parading yourself around the town.'

'I was young, but I still remember that. What an awful thing to say to your teenage daughter. And I mean honestly, I wasn't. I don't even think men were on my radar. I would find it hard even to speak to boys in school.' As children we start off all born the same, and then the layers are added over the years, she says. 'I know that those things that my dad said, that there were no skirts, no disco, no going out, you came in from school and that was it, you didn't go back out, those things definitely affected me. I think the strong male figures in your life growing up have a big impact on your own adult relationships.'

Five years ago, Emma got into a relationship with a man who, after the first six months, she discovered was lying to her repeatedly.

'I thought he was the business. What I know now is it was a pack of lies, but at the time, I totally fell for it. I was love-bombed.' In fact, what she didn't know was 'prostitutes, cocaine, drinker, affairs'. She didn't leave after she found out. 'It's nice to have somebody to do things with when you have children. He was the first man my children had met [since I had started dating again]. And I didn't want to fail at something again. I had failed at my marriage, I felt, Oh god, my mam has met this man, everybody knows I'm going out with him, am I going to fail again?'

She stayed in the relationship for three years. Finally, after yet another discovery of infidelity, a friend said to her, 'Emma you need to detach, and you need to get strong, and you need to realise this is toxic. This is not how people behave. That man has absolutely no respect for you. He doesn't know what love is.'

She left and she never went back, she says.

Of everything in her life, this relationship has been the most damaging to her, Emma adds. As is often the case with people who have found themselves in a toxic relationship, in the aftermath the self-reproach for being in the situation was a burden.

'I couldn't understand how I'd let somebody continuously treat me like that and gone back to them. Where was my self-respect, my own dignity? If you meet somebody in person you are more likely to know their background. My ex-boyfriend, I met him online, and I believed his bullshit for the first six months, because I didn't know anybody who knew him.'

Afterwards, she took some time off dating for the first time since her marriage had ended. She says now that maybe she originally went into dating too soon after her divorce. Instead, she worked on herself, and she was happy.

'I felt so relieved to be out of that relationship. I was able to just work, look after the kids, try to keep everything going in that sense. I took a lot of time on my own. And I walked, that would be my headspace. I was relieved to be able to sleep. When I was in that relationship, I used to wake all the time in the middle of the night, because I knew he was out drinking. I'd be logging into his Gmail to see what he was up to. Taking every opportunity to check his phone, text messages and even his call history. It's an awful way to live,' she says of such hypervigilance. 'I would nearly not go away myself for a weekend, thinking he'll definitely be out drinking and on coke, and out riding, and I need to be out too. I was so relieved. I'd a lovely Christmas. I spent all of it on my own, my girls went to their dad's house.'

After about six months, a friend called over one night and urged Emma to go back online, 'just go on till you see what's out there'. Rather than go back on the apps, she decided to try match.com, figuring if people were paying, they were more likely to be looking for what she was looking for – a relationship. Thirty-seven at the time, she changed her preferred age range to thirty-six to forty. She wanted to meet a man locally, so kept the kilometres range close.

Not long afterwards, she received a message from a man living half an hour away. 'A very standard message, no innuendo, no sexy nurse chat' – it had been an issue – 'just, *How're you getting on, how're you finding the pandemic? A normal chat.*'

They began messaging back and forth, but at a relaxed pace, no bombarding. 'He said, which they all say, *I'm thinking of coming offline, this is my number if you want to give me a text,*' she smiles.

They started to meet once a week. 'We got a takeaway coffee in the snow, the rain, the shite weather, we walked around a park, we had one text conversation a week, very briefly, just to arrange a coffee for that week, and we did this for, I'd say, six weeks. Taking it slowly and cautiously meant that I didn't even think of taking it further for a good few dates in. We didn't sleep together for a couple of months and that is definitely unusual in the era of online dating.'

She was honest with him, said that she could not afford to get hurt again, needed to take things slowly. 'I know who I am, I know that if you and me are having sex, then I am invested in something,' she told him. 'So we just took it really slowly. I didn't sleep with him for three months. Which would not be like me.'

What's different this time is that they are friends. She repeatedly uses the word 'respectful' about their relationship. He doesn't lavish her with showy gifts like the last person, but always has small, thoughtful things for her: flowers from his garden, her favourite chocolate bar, a book he mentioned she said she would also like to read, a vitamin drink she favours. Once, she mentioned that she would like to go to Barcelona, and the next time he came to visit, he had brought a book about the city.

They still don't speak every day. 'I might get a text message and it would say, *Hi Emma*. I love that, it's respectful. Everyone likes to hear their own name. I really like that he uses my name a lot. It's intimate, affectionate.'

She has never been in a relationship like this, she says. It is because of her experiences over the past eight years, however, that, 'I know how to behave in an adult relationship. And I'm very secure, because I don't think he's sleeping with other people. That's just not who he is. I know what's important to me, and what I want and need in a long-term partner. It's taken me a long time to be able to enjoy the everyday mundane with a partner.'

Emma had described herself as a Holy Joe as a child. I wonder how she feels about it now. 'It's still there and it's very important to me. Even though I am divorced, and I don't go to mass the way I would have gone, I would still go, I would still pray every day,' she says. 'I do believe in all of that, and I know a lot of people don't and that's fine, and I respect that.' It is important to her, nonetheless.

Marriage is also really important to her, she adds, explaining that she is a traditionalist, a stance informed by being a Catholic. 'And I know that that sounds a bit hypocritical, because I am divorced and I initiated that separation, but I would be a traditionalist. There are times where I would still look at other families where there's a mum and a dad and there's that pang of envy, even now, eight years later. And I will still always kind of be sad that

I don't have that. Whereas my friend who's not religious at all, she's like, "Oh that would never have even crossed my mind."'

'I know it sounds ridiculous, because I'm the one that's divorced, and who initiated it all. But that was because I do believe that regardless of everything that we're taught growing up, we should still be happy in life, and you're not going to live a life of misery because the Church tells you that you need to put up with it.'

That said, she thinks religion is important. 'We'll be old and decrepit, and what else will we have? Probably not much other than faith and prayer.'

She would get married again. 'I'm already thinking what engagement ring I'm going to be wearing,' she grins.

15

A Tinder Glitch

When she would meet someone she was interested in, Isobel would always hesitate before deciding whether to tell them she is from Sherkin Island. Sherkin is an island off the south-west coast of Ireland, roughly three miles long and with a population of about a hundred people. Izzy is shy, and not always in the mood for the inevitable reaction she knows will follow.

'Everyone is always like "wow",' she smiles, pottering about the wooden cabin in which she lives on an organic farm in west Cork. It's a beautiful green room with a piano in the corner. She's pouring us homemade cordial, wildflowers sit in a bottle on the table, her small dog fusses at our feet for a while before settling. 'No matter how alternative they are, or where they're from that's also interesting, everyone's like "cooool", an island.'

It seems like such a contained world, somehow unknowable, I say, telling her about my parents' stories of summers spent living on An Blascaod Mór, and the atmosphere after the last tourist boat had left in the evening. She gives me a direct look that quite clearly says don't be nonsensical: growing up in a place, day after day, gets you firmly into the non-magical, the prosaic.

I have known Izzy – as I always call her – since she was a teenager, and she was the same then as she is now. She looks like someone Winona Ryder might have played in her own teenage years, and while she is, as she says, shy, she's also very dry and funny.

Even as a fourteen-year-old, she could hold her own with adults. It's probably something to do with growing up in a small community on an island, she says when I point this out.

'As a teenager on the island I was around a lot of adults, working in the pub, and with tourists. Also, because my parents were strict and I wasn't allowed be on my *own* at home, I had to go with them when they went to their friends' houses. I was always around grown-ups.' She speculates now that it might have informed her relationships with men as an adult.

'My longest relationship has been with someone who's seventeen years older than me. I think growing up on Sherkin, being around people of all different ages, that made it okay to go out with someone with such a big age gap. When I was fifteen, I started going out with a guy for a while who was nineteen … now all my friends are in their thirties and forties.'

Izzy is in her late twenties and living on her own, something she loves.

'I still don't know what to say when someone's like, "where are you from?"' she grins. 'It depends who they are. I would say Sherkin if I'm trying to impress them,' she laughs, agreeing that this is because she knows they will be fascinated, a response her home place inevitably elicits. But she is not always keen to be landed with the attention. 'If I was a really confident person, I'd be telling everyone.'

Izzy grew up on Sherkin Island, the youngest of three siblings. Both her parents were originally from England: her mother moved there after spotting a sign on a noticeboard in university looking for someone to do some house-sitting. She never left. Her father was touring the west of Ireland with a traditional music group when he came to Sherkin. Knitting, fishing, sailing tours, mussel-farming, boatbuilding and home help are all amongst the various ways they have made a living.

Izzy lived on the island until she was seventeen, apart from a few years in Schull from the age of six when she attended the local primary school in Ballydehob, but would still return to Sherkin at weekends.

'It was completely different going to the mainland, being in a *normal* school in Ballydehob. Well, it was a hippy, Protestant school,' she qualifies. 'It was good to be around other kids my own age.' In the school on Sherkin, there had been twelve children in total, two teachers and two classrooms.

Days on the island could be lonely and boring. Her parents were strict about her movements, and so she was limited in how much time she could spend with the other children, often spending time at home instead.

'I'd just be wanting friends, and bored … I suppose I was crafty,' she shrugs. When she was with the other children, they would spend their time cycling around the island, exploring. You would live for the Easter or summer holidays, Izzy explains. 'When there were holiday home-owners around and all their kids would come down.'

There would be 'mad crushes' on the holiday-home kids. 'You'd go to the beach when you were ten, eleven, twelve, and be trying to match up. "Okay, who's going to kiss who?" One girl was really confident so it would be known who she fancied, and I suppose whoever else was left over, I'd have them.'

She was matched with a boy from Cork city one year, one from Bandon another summer. 'Just being so awkward,' she recalls. 'We'd go behind the castle, or we'd go to the beach, and it would be like, our turn to kiss.'

In secondary school on the mainland, Izzy was 'so ready to be around people', and reconnected with the best friend she had made during the years in primary school in Ballydehob. Her family became Izzy's mainland home. Each day she would bring an overnight bag, never knowing whether the weather would turn and she would be unable to return home by boat.

Izzy recalls how being an islander made her stand out. 'I definitely had this islander badge above my head. All the island kids did. Even my closest friends would be like, oh, the islander. And I'd think, but it's the same as the mainland, it's just hard to get places. It's like eight minutes on the boat, a stone's throw.'

There were teenage crushes, a boyfriend she didn't speak to for months, then kissed at the local disco – 'we kissed for forty-five minutes on the dance floor. It was only because he was also very shy, and we didn't know how to end it.' Then, in fifth and sixth year at school, Izzy had a boyfriend who came from a very wealthy family that, having lived abroad, had moved to the area. Her islander status intensified the normal teenage embarrassment.

'I was mortified to be an islander going out with him. His dad would drive down to the tiny fishing pier in his Range Rover, and my dad would come in his little orange fishing boat, *brrrrr*.' She mimes the loud noise of the engine, shaking with laughter at the memory. 'He was there to collect me from staying at their house for the weekend. Dead, I was just dead. He [the boyfriend] came to my house on the island once. We were together for two and a half years.'

Their family car smelled of fishing lines, and there were coils of fishing rope covered in seaweed in the boot, all sources of humiliation for a teenager trying to fit in. 'I remember my parents wanted to go for a drive one day when I was in secondary school. We went through Schull, and I literally was like ...' She mimes throwing herself on the floor, hiding. She stayed in the car when they went into the shop. At parent-teacher days she would worry about people seeing her hippy islander parents.

Now she is the complete opposite. 'I think my dad's *amaaaazing*; I *really* appreciate him. I'm into all the same stuff as my parents now anyway.'

As a teenager, though, she was unhappy living on the island. 'As soon as I got on the ferry and I was around other people, I was at home. I hated being on Sherkin because my parents were strict, it was boring, and our house was so cold and damp. It was just like "get me out of here", you know?'

During college in University College Cork, she stayed in the city on the weekends rather than return home. In the summer, she went back to the island and worked in the pub. This was much more preferable than being a teenager on the island. She would spend most of her time in the pub, which was fun, and her parents had by them decided she could do whatever she wanted. 'It was still a challenge to get to the mainland,' she adds.

She didn't move back to the island as an adult, but you get the impression that the life she had growing up has informed the priorities she now holds about where she wants to live. Place is paramount. Where, often, it is a type of place that will give people the lifestyle they are after (farm, island, small town), in Izzy's case only a very specific area will provide. 'That's all I know. I don't know what career I want, or how to make money, I just want to be here,' Izzy says of the stretch of west Cork coastline from Clonakilty to Rosscarbery – maybe as far as Leap she concedes which is the only area she would contemplate living, or where she feels at home.

It was the only decision that was clear. 'I really want to live in this place, everything else doesn't matter.'

It was the hardest thing about ending her last relationship, which is over about a year and a half when we first speak. 'The lifestyle suited me.' She had thought that in ending things, she would have to give that up too. Her therapist helped her realise she could have all the things that she was describing herself.

I ask her to identify the lifestyle, and she lists a number of things: live music in local pubs, a friend group which is all into the same things, on the same wavelength.

'Everyone goes to therapy, doesn't really drink alcohol, and that's kind of rare enough.' It is an attitude that prioritises life over work. It feels similar to west Clare, where she has friends in Lahinch. 'I like that the further west you go, you can go to the shop in whatever. I feel like, even in Clonakilty, but especially in cities, you have to look quite put together.' She does ceramics in Coolmountain – 'just pottering away with all these old ladies' – sits on the headland with her binoculars looking for whales and birds, hangs out with friends one to one. Growing up on Sherkin has instilled in her a need to be in nature. 'Sometimes when I walk and there's stuff on my mind, I just start singing. Especially if it's windy, because it's always windy on Sherkin, and no one can hear you. As an adult I'll find myself doing it without actively thinking about doing it. Walk and sing into the wind, really loudly.'

Of late, she has been returning to the island more frequently, helping her father – whose restorations of traditional boats are somewhat legendary in the area – with some work, then went walking about the place. 'It was just magical,' she concedes wistfully. 'I missed it so much. I thought, I'm home. I love this place so much.'

When her last relationship ended, she waited a while before beginning to date again. Then summer came, and she got the burst of energy she says she always does at that time of year for these things.

'I'm suddenly full of energy to meet people, I'm on a mission,' she laughs. She joined Tinder, specifically to see if one person she liked was on it. 'And to see if they were single. I know where he lives, so I set it at a ten-kilometre perimeter.' She bursts out laughing again. 'I found him, but he didn't swipe me back.'

She then broadened her radius on Tinder to twenty kilometres. 'Because if I meet someone from Bandon, we're probably not going to have anything in common.'

Occasionally she set it to sixty kilometres, 'which is Cork city. Because I'd be willing to meet someone who just lived somewhere else but is willing to move here and do this. A few of my friends' partners were like that.'

She prefers to meet people in real life. 'But I'm so shy, that's my problem.' The pandemic didn't help. A number of her friends are against Tinder for moral reasons, she confesses. 'Oh, Tinder's not very ethical. It trains your mind to disregard people, it doesn't prioritise being kind to people. It's not *my* take on it,' she adds dryly.

'Isobel, I can't *believe* you're still on Tinder, isn't it like a game?' A friend said to her a while ago.

'I don't care,' she shrugs. It's hard pushing yourself out there in real life sometimes. 'If you're confident, you just swing by, call 'round to someone, that's how you get to know people.'

Every so often she would make forays back on Tinder, full of hope. They would never last. 'When you download it again freshly or reopen your profile after not being on for a while, you're excited. That doesn't last too long. You get to the end of the stack of twenty kilometres, or even sixty kilometres, very quickly. Because I would know what I'm looking for, I could literally go like this,' she mimes rapid swiping.

Living alone can allow social media to take up a bigger part of your life than it might do if there was someone else there to, if nothing else, simply shame you off your phone. If there's no one there to comment on how much time you are spending scrolling, it's easy to go down the rabbit hole and spend hours online. Lockdown, and its combination of dead time and isolation, simply compounded this: at one point Izzy deleted WhatsApp because of the amount of time she was spending on it.

'I definitely got into chats with people where I'm on my phone constantly communicating with them. Because I'm like that with WhatsApp, and if you meet someone else who's also like that, you could have a full-blown relationship that's just over the phone. Sending each other videos throughout the day ... it's like you're hanging out together.'

She did meet someone else who was like that, a man from the midlands, over three hours away by car. They would communicate for hours over the phone. When they met up in person there was an initial dissonance as she adjusted to the real-life him, rather than the online version. 'We were chatting a lot on WhatsApp, and then when I met him I liked him, but he was quite different to how I imagined he would be, because obviously you have this picture of them in your mind.'

These false expectations created out of online intimacy are something Dr Nicola Fox Hamilton noticed during her research in the past two years when interviewing daters during lockdown. She terms it hyper-personal communication.

'What happens is [that] when you're communicating through text, you're missing all the body-language cues, not fully seeing what somebody is like. You already liked their online pictures, which means you had an initially positive impression of them, so you view everything after that with something of a rosy glow, kind of a confirmation bias. What can happen is [that] you begin filling in the gaps in your knowledge about them with more positive information, you build quite an idealised impression. Also, because you're online, you might share more information, because it's easier to. It can build quite quickly into this very intense, emotional, intimate sort of relationship online. You haven't actually met yet. The longer you're communicating without meeting, the more likely that is to happen. Particularly through text. Texting is much more likely to build that sense of intimacy.'

It was a Tinder glitch that brought them together, Izzy smiles. He was beyond her radius, but somehow appeared on her feed. Tinder does that sometimes, she shrugs. 'I liked the look of him, and we had brilliant chats.'

As chance would have it, he was coming to nearby Kinsale in a few weeks, for a couple of months of work. On their first date, Izzy took him to the headland near the organic farm where she lives. 'We had fancy pizza for takeaway. He was blown away because it was an incredible evening, West Cork is so beautiful.' There is adjusting to be done, she smiles, when you meet someone in real life after copious amounts of online interaction. They broke up: the distance between where they both live was tricky, she points out. Apart from the logistical issues, it can impede getting to know someone if the bulk of a relationship happens in one person's place, she says. There are gaps in your knowledge of them if you don't see them in their place. 'Our relationship was in my world, not his.' But in the months afterwards, she kept thinking about him.

They decided to meet again, in a more neutral venue, and had a weekend away, which was 'the most fun weekend I've had in years'.

And then Izzy got pregnant. He was supportive, but also shocked. It had not been in either of their plans. She considered an abortion, made several appointments. 'It went as far as being in hospital with the last appointment,' she says. When she began crying, the nurse gently told her, 'I don't think we should do it today, I don't think you're ready to do it.' A counsellor came in to talk to her. 'The service in the hospital was so brilliant and kind and sensitive and human. I've never been treated with such care,' she recalls.

'In the end I just couldn't do it. And as soon as I made that decision I was over the moon. And I made that decision thinking that I might be a single parent from the beginning. I wasn't sure.'

But since then, he has been completely and utterly on board. He's moving shortly, they will live in west Cork.

She's not exactly sure how things will pan out with the relationship, but 'I can make it work,' she says, certainty ringing in her voice. She means having her baby, not the relationship. They are happy when they are together, she says, there are no issues, only that they still haven't had the chance to spend much time together as he is finishing up some work before he moves to west Cork.

'After all the tumult of the on-and-off relationship followed by the surprise pregnancy, any strong feelings we were developing are on the back burner. We're having a baby but taking it slowly. Isn't that often the way anyway?

'I feel like the luckiest person in the world. I feel lucky in a sense that that's where we're at. It's like, there's way less expectation now than [for] a married couple having a child. There's room for all eventualities, and that they're all okay. At least that's how I see it.'

She used to not tell people they had met on Tinder. 'I'm a little bit of a romantic, old-fashioned, and there's something much nicer to having a story as to how you met.' But she realises now there is a story to how they met. The glitch on Tinder that brought them together.

Part Four
Coming Home

16

How Are *You* Single?

It's a beautiful sunny winter's day, and the three of us are sitting in a line on a bench by the sea in Salthill, clutching hot drinks. We've avoided the busy waterside boardwalk itself – 'We'd have to keep giving the Galway hello,' Lisa had said with a laugh, explaining that this is when you see someone you know, but rather than stop and chat, you give them the nod and smile. Instead, we're across the road in a small park. It's still early days of emerging from lockdown, and everyone feels more comfortable outside.

Lisa and Sarah grew up near each other, Lisa in the city, Sarah in a suburb of Galway, but before today they hadn't known each other beyond a vague mutual awareness from 'around the place'. Their stories chimed, however, and I had asked if they would be willing to meet with me together for a second interview.

Both women have lived abroad for some time, Lisa in New York where she worked for several years before travelling around Australia; Sarah in London for a decade with regular work-related travel further afield. They have each returned to live in the place where they grew up.

Both women have known since they were small that they didn't want children.

'I don't really talk about it with people, so it's great to talk to you about it now,' Sarah says, turning to Lisa with a smile.

Sarah is forty, with the dark hair and pale skin considered typical of the west coast of Ireland. She's wearing lilac winged sunglasses and a beautiful, pale checked coat. Currently, she is taking a break from work to consider her next move, having stepped back from a creative role with an international company.

Lisa, thirty-six, runs her own PR company. Tall and athletic, she has arrived on her bike in leopard-print jeans, a bomber jacket and bright pink lipstick. Her eight-year-old dog, Toby, complete with a jaunty little dickie bow, sits in the front basket. That morning, like most days, she has swum in the sea. It was six degrees, so cold she finished with a run afterwards to warm up.

Lisa lives in her own house, while Sarah is currently living with her parents, having seen out the pandemic in the family home. She is now hoping to buy a house in Galway, she thinks, if she can find a way to make her career work. Both women have been single for several years.

'How are *you* single?' is a question that comes up a lot. Ostensibly it's a compliment, but actually it can feel quite loaded if you're on the receiving end. How are YOU single. The implication is that if you were half as fabulous as you appear to be, you wouldn't be single, so what's really wrong? Can you really be that great after all, the questions seems to suggest.

'How are *you* single?' Sarah adds contemplatively, nodding her head. It's been said to her too.

The 2016 census found that younger counties tended to have more single people, older counties more married and widowed people. Galway County, excluding the city, had a 41 per cent rate of single people and, in terms of nationwide figures, a slightly older population.

Lisa moved home as the recession was beginning, Sarah more recently, just after the pandemic had begun. Both are on the dating apps sporadically and take a break when it all gets a bit exhausting.

'I put myself back on the dating apps,' Sarah says now of her recent return online, with the sigh and slight roll of the shoulders that suggests reluctant effort, and which so often greets this statement. Back on the apps. Sigh.

She tends to try for a couple of months, then comes off again, a very normal pattern. 'It's typical for people to do it in waves,' Lucy Rand, co-founder of Muddy Matches dating site, says. 'You put yourself out there, go on a few dates, and if it doesn't work out you kind of need to take stock, have a breather, and get on with the rest of your life that isn't about always trying to find someone. When I used to online date myself, I did it in batches.'

Dating as life admin, a chore, is a characterisation of the experience that comes up repeatedly.

Lisa: 'It's an effort for me.'

Sarah, nodding agreement: 'It's such an effort.'

Lisa: 'I have to give it ten minutes a day. I don't even get excited.'

Sarah: 'The slog.'

Have the apps taken the fun out of dating, made it simply one more item on the to-do list? Dr Fox Hamilton explains the almost-contradiction of the online dating experience. 'A substantial majority of people who have online dated are relatively positive about it. And at the same time, a lot of them don't enjoy it,' she explains. 'So, they're positive about the options it gives, that it opens up a pool of new people, that they have more control over it, that it fits in with their lifestyle, can be more efficient, or at least it gives you the feeling that it is, I'm not sure if it actually is. A lot of time goes into the process of filtering and everything to get to a date, and most first dates aren't successful. It is so mainstream; it is the most likely way to meet a new partner now. Everybody feels that it's probably the way you should be meeting a new partner, or at least trying to.'

The vast majority of people will do it for a while, get tired, leave and come back, she explains.

'Up to seven, eight or more times over. Some people in my research have been doing it for almost twenty years,' she says, adding that in this case they may have met a long-term partner, then after the relationship ended gone back online. While it's viewed as positive in terms of convenience and providing more options, the actual experience is not always positive.

'Every so often I'd be like, Right, that's it, I'm fucking doing this. All guns blazing,' Sarah says ferociously, then laughs. 'And then it just feels so alien, I think because I came from a small town where you didn't have to do that. Because if you liked someone, you were *going* to see them in town. You were *going* to end up in the same pub. You just kind of learnt to flirt on the street, d'you know what I mean? In the wild, like.'

Before she moved to New York on her own when she was twenty, Lisa had had a few teenage relationships in Ireland. She couldn't get over the confidence and forwardness of men in America. 'You could be literally walking down the street and a guy would come up to you and say, "Hey, how's it going?" Just strike up a conversation. And not in that way where you'd be like, "Just piss off," like when lads are badgering you,' she laughs. 'It was so natural, so surreal. It just doesn't happen here.'

She loved the lightness of casual dating in New York. That it was understood that it didn't have to mean anything, but not in a way that made people disposable. Just 'no big deal' if you didn't want a second date.

In contrast, in Ireland, she finds there are two narratives available to women when dating. Either women want to get married and have children (and they want to trap men into that), or they just want to have sex. There's nothing in between, so you can't casually date, because people are like, 'No, you'll want more. It has to be on the terms of what the man perceives you to be. It's so draining.'

Every man she has talked to has asked her what she is looking for. They mean sex or a relationship, she clarifies. 'I had to take some time to realise how I wanted to answer that. Obviously, I wasn't going to say, "I'm looking for a husband." I haven't even met this man. I decided, okay, I'm not going to say that I want something casual, because I don't. I'm not in the mood for just going around having sex with people. If I was in the mood for that, that would be fine, but I'm not. I know what I want: a connection, and a relationship with someone who has the same core values and moral outlook as me in life. I didn't want to get too heavy with him, but that was my answer back.'

Sarah lived in London for ten years. 'I've been asked out more when I'm on my *holidays* in New York, than I have ever been in my entire life in London,' she laughs. 'London is very like, we're all too cool for everything. I can't even show that you're attractive, because I'm too cool, I don't need that in my life.'

While there, she developed her one-drink rule to avoid endless evenings spent with a person you knew within minutes of arriving you were not interested in.

'I'll know within the first five seconds. Yes or no. If I am texting someone and saying let's meet up, I say, *I hope you don't mind, but I have a thing where I only have one drink with someone.*' It avoids becoming embroiled in the emotional labour of a date. 'What would happen is I would feel really bad for this person and try and coax them out of their shell. Then I'd be like, what am I doing? It's not my job to make this person better for their next date. For fuck's sake, stop being such an Irish mammy about it.'

Returning from London, Sarah was surprised to find when she asked around that Tinder was the preferred app. 'In London, only psychopaths use Tinder,' she jokes. 'It's always about staying ahead of the game, so you leave the absolute weirdos to the last. Here, it seemed like everyone was using Tinder. And I was like, is that not just for sex?' She has since moved to Hinge and Bumble.

Lisa is on Hinge, having found Tinder to be 'the most disgusting place on the planet', she shudders. 'I've never experienced anything like that. I remember a guy saying, "Are you sure you're thirty-four, because you look a lot older?" It's like this cesspit. I was getting all these dick pics, or messages like *ure hot.*'

She was twenty-seven when she returned home. The recession was just hitting. 'It was weird adjusting at the start. I found the smallness claustrophobic. I loved the anonymity being away, and I also loved that it was non-judgemental. I still find Ireland very judgey like, just in terms of the small-mindedness, and how afraid people are to live their lives. They say stuff to you like, "Oh you're so braaaaave."'

Online dating had begun, but she was removed from it at that point. 'I was still meeting friends of a friend. It was all people that I knew through other people. Online dating seemed very foreign to me.'

She was twenty-eight when she first tried online dating and lasted two weeks. 'I hated it so much. These men had no conversation, you could tell they were sending the same messages to every girl. It's weird, it just felt quite attacking, almost like a strategy. Like you know in the school yard when you're young: oh I'll be mean to her and then she'll like me.'

At that point, she did feel some embarrassment. 'I definitely had some shame around being single at different points in my life. I think it's because it's often ingrained subliminally in the language of society. Oh, you're on your own, solo, single. Obviously, we'd all love to be in a really lovely, committed relationship, where you get on really well with somebody, and you connect with them. But I would rather not be in one that is not right. Because that is the saddest and loneliest place you've ever been in.'

After a three-year relationship ended, she went back online, thinking 'I need to be more proactive about meeting someone'. This time she lasted two days on Tinder. 'Guys sending you rotten messages, very sexually forward. *I'd say you're mad for it*, stuff like that. Grotesque.'

She reflects now that this kind of thing probably compounded what shame she felt, as if by being in such company, it somehow reflected upon her. 'Oh my god, is this all there is? But then I think, no it's not the dregs, because I'm on here, and I'm feckin' fabulous. This is how people meet now. So I stopped freaking myself out with it.'

I ask Lisa and Sarah what they think is behind the impulse on the part of men sending nude pictures.

'I feel like it's a power thing,' Sarah says.

Lisa agrees, and adds, 'I think it's a total lack of sexual experience as well. They are so sexually inexperienced in real life. They're big talk online because they've got this kind of cover, this security thing.'

The calibre of man on Hinge is vastly different. 'There's no smut, there isn't any sexual innuendo. Conversation is instantaneous. It's not just, hey, how are you? They'll ask probing questions.'

Of recently going back on the apps, Sarah says with a smile, 'I'd say there was some sort of global alert that a new person had arrived on, 'because the next day it was 197 people, and then it went up to 1,000.'

'I was laughing, because I thought there's definitely not a thousand people who are interested in me. Maybe it's that they just all swipe right. I think I'm seeing a lot of people from quite far away, like Cork and Limerick.'

'Men and women behave completely differently in terms of who they swipe right on, and connect with,' says Dr Fox Hamilton. 'Men are more likely to swipe right on more people. Women are pickier. That translates offline as well. Women tend to have higher standards. It's possibly from evolutionary psychology, where we want someone who's going to stick around and help. It's also societal needs, perhaps, where women didn't have the resources and so on. But as a result, men swipe right on a lot more women, even ones that they're not *that* interested in. And women swipe right on a lot fewer. And so men are sending quite a few responses to people, or initial responses to women. Particularly when a woman joins an app, and is remotely attractive, she's going to get tonnes of responses. She picks the best of those. So her standards go up, at least initially. She only responds to a few that look really good.'

Men who are getting a small number responses on the apps start swiping even more. Conversely, as women get even more matches their bar gets ever higher.

'It's this vicious circle where men are sending out so many of these messages that are just like *hey*. The median character length of first messages from men to women on Tinder is twelve characters. And a quarter of men send six characters or fewer. That's literally just *hey*, or *hello*, or *what's up*. With women's it's around 122 characters.'

Sarah describes the abundance of choice as bringing home how few men there were who she might be interested in.

'If you're in these apps where you've to swipe and you're at, like, a hundred and something and you haven't come across a single person, you just feel like you've spent two hours of your life self-affirming that you're never going to find someone.'

She set her age range from around mid-thirties to about fifty. Lisa had from twenty-eight. 'I have to change that. Because actually 28-year-olds and me ...' she trails off, laughing.

'I can't cope,' Sarah smiles, rolling her eyes.

'No, I can't cope either. I thought maybe just once or twice for sex. But I can't actually listen to them. They're so annoying,' Lisa laughs. 'They're taking selfies.'

Both women have experienced ghosting.

'It's the *pittttss*,' Sarah smiles and groans.

Lisa describes meeting a man a few years ago at a workshop. He instigated their conversation, found her afterwards on Instagram, and they began messaging.

'We got on so well, and I was attracted to him. I thought, wow, this is great.' They arranged to go on a date that Saturday daytime, which she always prefers for the first meeting. 'We were texting all week, and then on the Saturday he just didn't text me. It was so weird. That was literally it.'

She texted him, 'Hey what's the story?' He didn't reply.

'And then a few months later he started liking my pictures again on Instagram. What's wrong with people? I've gone on loads of dates with people who I haven't liked. If they ask would you like to go on a second date, I say I had a really nice time today, but it just isn't for me, and just leave it at that.'

It left her feeling deflated. 'We met, we got on really well, I was attracted to him. And you know, you're a girl then, you're like, this is going to be great. I was so disappointed. And then I was like, what a weirdo.'

The smallness of the community in which they're living affects them both positively and negatively. When examined for urban and rural areas separately, the data from the 2016 census showed that there was a higher proportion of single people in urban areas (44.5 per cent) than in rural ones (35.4 per cent). 'Tiny,' Lisa says of the options. 'You'd be lucky to get four dates a month.'

'I feel like I see the same faces on each app, you get familiar even without seeing them around in real life,' Sarah adds, laughing.

Being back where she grew up can be hard, Sarah reflects. Unlike Lisa, whose return to Galway wasn't a given, she always thought of moving home, used all her holidays from work to visit. Now though, friends who lived here have moved on. Making new ones can be hard. 'I feel like a new kid at school. And I never was a new kid at school. But I just feel like I've lost a lot of my Irishness.'

Beyond dating, it is a different experience simply existing as a single person here than it was in London.

'I'm used to being out on my own, I've travelled so much. Going to the pub, having a glass of wine on my own. But there's something about doing it in your hometown that feels quite vulnerable. I suppose it's just showing me what I think it might look like. "Oh Sarah, I saw her the other day, she was drinking *on her own*." It's my own weirdness. I don't think that about anyone else,' she smiles. 'Who cares, really? You know?'

When the pubs opened after one of the lockdowns, she went one day with her book to sit outside with a pint.

'An old friend of mine passed, she was with her kid. And she was like, "*What* are you *doing*?" The judgement on her face. She was kind of disgusted. Like, are you not mortified? Couldn't compute it. And I thought, that's what I've been afraid of. There are people in my life who are kind of judgemental. What do you think single people do? Am I supposed to stay indoors all the time and not enjoy myself?' she laughs.

In 2016 more than a quarter of males (26.3 per cent) in the 40–49 age group were single, while amongst women 23.6 per cent were single. There have traditionally been more unmarried men than women in this age group but that gap is narrowing: over the twenty-year period from 1996 to 2016 the percentage of single women in this age group has more than doubled from 11 per cent to almost 24 per cent. The data for the urban and rural areas differs noticeably. In rural areas only 16.6 per cent of women in this age group were single compared with 28 per cent in urban areas, while for men the figures were 22.3 per cent and 28.9 per cent respectively.

In the 40–49 age group, figures from the 2016 census showed that Galway had one of the highest percentages of people married, at 71.3 per cent, lower only than Meath and Kildare.

For Lisa, most of her friends are having kids now, which changes the nature of being single. 'It can be challenging. Their life fundamentally changes, so everything goes on to the schedule of the person with the child. You have to meet them in their house, with their child, or everything has to be during the day.'

Despite the sensitivity you might expect around such a personal matter, they have both found that in fact people feel no compunction about bringing up motherhood and not wanting to have a child. It's as if they find it hard to accept that this is a definitive decision, Sarah explains.

'No you definitely will, aaaaah no, you'll change your mind.'

'But you're so nurturing.'

'You'll definitely want children. You'd be a great mother.'

'You're so kind.'

'When you meet the right one, you're going to have children.' (Pitying head tilt.)

All are things people say on hearing that you do not want to have children. Both women point out that this is not the case for men who do not want to have children.

'For some people, it's unnatural for a woman to say she doesn't want kids, it's like you're going against nature,' Lisa says, adding that she is always delighted for others when they announce they're having children. The 'it's not that I don't like kids, I just don't want them for myself disclaimer'.

Now, early into dating someone, Lisa will bring up the fact that she does not want children.

'I don't have any shame about it, whereas before I would have had a little bit. When you move into your thirties, for some people there's a script to life in Ireland. College, meet someone, buy a house, the car, have the big wedding, then straight away children. I didn't have the urge to do any of that.'

Sometimes men will react in a way that feels judgemental when she tells them she does not plan on becoming a mother, but on other occasions they are relieved, as if she has given them an option they hadn't quite allowed themselves.

'It's like there's this queue for life, and you join that queue, but nobody thinks about the other queues. That if you're experiencing life with a partner, you don't *have* to get married, you don't *have* to have children – that's a total choice. And there are loads of other choices. But in Ireland those choices are kind of seen as secondary. It's like, but are you *really* happy?'

She strikes me as someone who has a lovely life: a job she enjoys, the autonomy of running her own business, friends, but also a person who is comfortable going out on their own. She mentions a show she went to see recently, a restaurant she likes to visit solo.

'I still would like to go out with my adult friends and do something as adults. But having children and a family is all-consuming and I appreciate that, so both parties have to realise that you are now on different schedules. It can be hard on the friendship, as you both gravitate more towards where you are at in your life. For me that pull is a little bit towards friends who don't have children. Because you've more in common at that time. I have loads of friends too that don't want families. A lot of my friends want an adult life, without children. We are definitely the first generation to be living openly this way and talking about it.'

The proximity of your past in a smaller community isn't necessarily a bad thing. Sarah describes recently seeing an ex-boyfriend from before she left Galway and realising she is utterly over him.

'It brought up a lot of stuff. The beauty of a small-enough town is that you kind of are forced to deal with those feelings. They come up every time you see someone. Or you're forced to see that person with another person. So in one way, it's really good, because you can't bottle those feelings which exist. You have to get through them. Whereas when you're away, you're not confronted with that.'

'I was like, Jesus, it's been so long, and I have absolutely no love whatsoever for this person. If I had lived here that whole time, would I have come to that conclusion way earlier? It would have been nice to realise my progression a long time ago.'

Things are changing in terms of the choice out there. 'It's falling into really weird categories for me, of say the 27-year-old guy to thirty-four, and then older,' Lisa laughs. 'So you either have this single guy that, you know, might be great in a few years' time, or you're getting the second-time-rounders, whose relationships have broken down.'

'I'm on the app. But I don't have any pressure rushing me,' Lisa says.

'I was just going to say. That's the fucking beauty of where we are,' Sarah replies.

'I have my own life and my own money. I don't need a man, but I would love one to share my life with,' Lisa adds.

17

I Never Want to Meet
People in the Pub

Of everyone I interview, Timmy stands out for one particular reason. He is the only person I speak to for this book who professes to not just like but actively prefer using dating apps to meet people, rather than finding them in real life.

'I don't do pubs or clubs, so I'd rather have a conversation with someone,' he says, explaining that he doesn't drink. 'That's why I like the apps. Because I have good conversations with people.' This is also an outlier – the difficulty of conversation on the apps is an issue regularly mentioned by other interviewees.

Timmy is thirty-six, a model and an actor who also runs a photography business when the two former jobs are quiet. He is veritably bursting with get-up-and-go positivity. He tells me about slow moments on set

recently, when he would chat to crew members, dissuad-
ing them from smoking, encouraging press-ups. One guy
went from ten cigarettes to one a day, he says proudly.
Timmy is a fan of Tony Robbins, the American life coach.
When his father became ill, he came home from Australia
– to help his family, 'do the right thing' – to the town in
Kerry where he grew up and now lives once again. The
day we meet, he has travelled from home to Cork to
bring a friend to hospital. He tells me about his dog, who
he calls his 'baby', shows me pictures, describes how
when he was living abroad he would call his parents, but
mainly to speak to the dog.

His parents met in the town Timmy grew up in, they lived
around the corner from each other. After coming home to
help look after his father he fell back in love with Kerry, with
the beaches.

You get the sense of someone who wears life lightly.
Timmy is very sure of who he is, is happy in himself,
doesn't overthink things. This, it seems, also translates into
an ability to take online dating very much in his stride. He
is uniformly positive about the apps.

Having some kind of criteria as you wade into the dating
apps is a necessity that is regularly mentioned. A baseline
of what you are after. Timmy is very clear on what he looks
for in a woman. 'Ideally, a woman who doesn't drink, loves
her exercise, has nice teeth. If I was to meet someone, and
they didn't look after their teeth, or they weren't hygienic,
good luck to you.'

He politely but briskly dispenses with any possible
downsides I put to him about online dating in a smaller

community. Why would it be awkward meeting someone you know from a small community on a dating app? He's talked online to a girl who grew up near him, she knows his brother.

The intimacy of a smaller community, the lack of anonymity, isn't something that bothers him when it comes to being on the apps. Why would he care about people knowing he is online dating? 'So many people worry about what people think of them. I don't care what people's perception of me is because I'm comfortable in what I do. I love life.' In fairness, he's right. As my research goes on I notice an age-related difference in attitudes to the simple fact of online dating, not even getting into the experience of it, but the sense of shame or oddness of just having to turn to it. The older a person, the more keenly they may feel this, to the point of recoiling in horror (this is more likely to be someone who is not single, and who met their partner years ago, before smartphones were even in existence). The younger somebody is, the more likely they are to view it as a given that this will be how they meet someone.

'For me anyway, the apps are really good,' Timmy adds.

It's all about the conversation. 'I have the gift of the gab, so if someone doesn't want to talk to me, I'll talk to someone else,' he grins. 'You will be forever known as the Kerry guy who never shut the fuck up,' the guys on a recent set told him, he laughs. As such, the apps facilitate this.

In fact, a reluctance to keep chatting is his one criticism of online dating in Ireland. In Canada he found people were more willing to have a conversation on the phone. It would typically be two or three weeks of chatting before they would meet. Here, give it two days and people are suggesting meeting up.

The minimum he likes to talk to someone before meeting is two weeks. As a teetotaller, his ideal first date is either a hike or a trip to the beach, something his home place easily facilitates.

'If someone doesn't look like they'd be into hiking, I swipe left. If someone looks like they're fit, and they have nice teeth and all that, then I'll swipe right, and then we'll have a conversation. I'll just say, so tell me about yourself.' (It is at this point in our conversation that I realise I've started discreetly holding my hand over my mouth – Timmy and I would never have made it off the apps.)

There's a certain upfront, cut-to-the-chase-ness of online dating that seems to suit Timmy's personality. Being on a dating app is often compared to having one's own shopfront with the self as product, best side out. Maybe if you are clear about what you want, à la Timmy, it cuts through some of this? It is like a clear list of boxes to be ticked, its own form of authenticity in a heavily curated world. This is what I want, this is what is important to me, therefore this is who I am. Who are you? Do we match?

'In the pub, it's five-minute conversations: "oh he's hot, she's hot." On the phone you'd chat to someone for so long … you find out if they're similar to you, have the same goals.

'I never want to meet people in the pub because I think, people I meet there, it's never going to last. You meet when you're kind of drunk.' In fact, he thinks meeting someone online offers a better chance of a proper conversation and therefore the opportunity to get to know that person in more depth. Timmy is extremely himself at all times. For him, this makes online interactions more likely to be genuine than IRL meetings in a pub, potentially clouded by alcohol.

Sometimes when he tells people he doesn't drink or smoke, they'll respond with something along the lines of 'oh that's very noble of you', mocking him. It doesn't bother him. He thinks it's a waste of money and he'd rather do other things. He doesn't want children: when he tells women this, the next day a lot of them have unmatched, he smiles, which he likes. It's an honest transaction.

Timmy speaks in almost fond terms of Tinder, which he has been using for years, like it's a stalwart in our lives, a kind of heritage brand. 'It reminds me of Vodafone, it is the Vodafone of the online dating world.' He knows it's considered largely a hook-up app but that hasn't been his experience – in fact the opposite is true. He finds it a good way to start properly getting to know someone.

He would typically go on the app daily. 'Sometimes when I've nothing to do, I just like looking around, swiping.' Typically he talks to two or three women at a time. He has started meeting a woman he was talking to and she's lovely.

Always, he bases his right swipes on the presence of certain things in a woman's pictures. 'If they don't have nice teeth, if I don't see any exercise, hiking or something like that, if I see someone in the pub, with a drink in their hand: no. Everyone has their little thing. My three things are exercise, looking after yourself, and nice teeth.'

Timmy smiles. His teeth are perfect.

18

I Knew *of* Him

Growing up on a small dairy farm which her brother now runs in Glengarry, ten minutes from Listowel – a market town in North Kerry – Edaein never had a boyfriend. 'I don't know if it's because of the fact when you're from a small town you know everyone in such detail already, whether it's by proxy or directly. Listowel is small, we all know each other, I never had any romantic dealings at all,' she smiles, shaking her head and her shiny new bob.

When Edaein went to college in Galway, it was the same thing, and it began to weigh on her. 'Oh my god, do boys not *like* me?' she thought.

She can see now that as everyone around her started to couple up, it began to affect her confidence. 'All my friends would have gotten with one of the lads from home or something, and I never had that. Texting fellas, or you'd have a fella at a disco, things like that. So then I put kind of a mark on myself that I was either not attractive, or there was something wrong with me. I think that has filtered through my life.'

Now twenty-seven, it wasn't until she went home again for a year out after several years of studying, at the age of twenty-one, that she met someone, Senan, her boyfriend. 'First and only boyfriend,' she laughs.

'Went to college, there wasn't a sinner there.' She came home and, as yet unsure of what she wanted to do with her life, got a job in SuperValu for a year.

'He was on the floor, and I was on the tills. And my brother was the manager,' she adds with a laugh.

After the year out, she moved to Dublin to do a Master's degree. The distance was hard, and Edaein and Senan broke up. Her friends urged her to get out there, get on Tinder. 'I tried. I *couldn't do it*. I don't know *how* people do it,' she laughs and squirms. She was appalled at the thought of having to strike up communication with someone online about whom she knew nothing. Where to even start? 'This texting thing, I was like, *no*. All my friends said go on a date with someone, but I just physically couldn't. I thought, "This is so hard. What do I talk to them about?"'

This knowing of a person – of having a sense of their background – is important to her. She likes the fact that even though she didn't know Senan well, he was from the same town. 'When you're from a small town … I would have known of him anyway.' Not much *about* him, she adds – he was the year below her in school – but *of* him. This makes a difference.

Edaein is chatty. She's a journalist, talking to people is part of her job. It's not an inability to strike up a conversation with someone that is the issue with online dating. It is, rather, a sense of familiarity, a shared back catalogue and a similar frame of reference that only someone who is from the same place would have, which offers her reassurance. 'I knew who his mother was. I *really* like that. Because – and this isn't in a bad way –but you'd know a family's backstory when you're down here. And it's not that it gives comfort but, when you meet someone and you're starting from scratch, you don't know anything about them, *nothing*, there's no familiarity there, and that's really hard. When I hear some of my friends talking about dating now, that is one of the hard parts.'

The break-up lasted six months, and then they did long distance between Dublin and Kerry. Edaein was building a career in journalism, but she was beginning to find Dublin stressful. 'I felt like I was constantly hot. That's the only way that I can explain it, I felt that I was constantly sweaty.' Always on the move, paying exorbitant rent, living pay cheque to pay cheque, beginning to consider going freelance, but concerned that the uncertainty that that would involve would have been made more difficult by the expense of living in Dublin. No other option seemed possible, however. If she wanted to pursue the career of her choice, she needed to be in Dublin.

When the pandemic began, she was living in a small apartment with two other girls. Working from home would have been dreadful. She moved back to Listowel, to her parents' home on the farm where she had grown up, and like so much of the world began to work remotely, an option previously unthinkable.

Edaein's story is part of a wider one, of the wave of internal migration set off by Covid-19. Where typically the direction of migration was rural to urban, and women just like Edaein left to find work while male siblings inherited the farm, the pandemic changed the direction of the flow of movement to some extent. It opened up new possibilities, allowed for a return, or first-time move, to more rural parts of the country, without compromising career choice.

'Every type of job that could be done remotely was done remotely during the pandemic,' explains Joanne Mangan of Grow Remote, a not-for-profit organisation. 'Which opened up industries that wouldn't really have considered remote working. That has been hugely transformative.' Where we work, the source of work, has changed. The pandemic transformed that.

It could be transformative not just in how people work, but with wider consequences in the general socio-economic landscape of rural and urban Ireland. 'I grew up in rural Ireland, my hometown is in Mayo – no way would I have been able to get a job there. I left and went to Dublin. I'm in Athenry now, I never would have dreamed I could get a job there, I would have assumed I would have to move to Dublin,' Joanne adds.

For Edaein, things were different when she returned home in early 2020 than how it had been that year after college when she met Senan. Then, everyone was scattered, now it felt almost as it had when they were all living at home as teenagers.

'Back then, everyone was doing different things. Some were still in college, others off working.' Now all her friends were coming home. 'It was weird. We were all around, it was like being fifteen again, drinking in my friend's shed.'

In fact, the pandemic opened up Edaein's working world. 'What's weird is that moving home has actually made my world a lot bigger than it was even when I was in Dublin. When I was in Dublin, it was very much insular, you were dealing with your industry in that particular city. Whereas I've come home to Kerry and I have been opened up to so many more opportunities. So I'm very positive about that, and a lot of my friends are as well.'

'It is *so* rural,' she says of where she lives, 'and I work daily for people in London. Before the pandemic, I would not have realised that I could be based from home and be employed by the places that I've worked for.'

Being able to live at home in her parents' house is another bonus. 'I think that's something I was always envious of in Dublin. People who were from the city, they could live with their parents and enjoy the city without the stress of rent.' Now at home, she and a lot of her friends are enjoying the same situation.

She adds that she thinks the pandemic has pushed people to settle down much earlier than they might otherwise have. 'They're buying dogs or a house or something like that. We'd nothing to do, so people just think sure this is nice, I'll just keep going with this.'

It made things much easier for her relationship. They had both always wanted to stay in the place they were from and now they could. A partner from the same place you grew up in isn't for everyone. She acknowledges how the continuity might be unappealing for some. It is difficult to make a stamp with your adult self on people who knew you growing up. 'I can see how it would hinder people. You see these people you've grown up with all your life. They know a certain version of you that they have in their heads from when you were teenagers. You're a completely different person now. It's very hard to separate the person you were from who you are now, it's very difficult for the person on the other side, for lads around here maybe, to do that. I can see that kind of hindered me in the past, and I was kind of lucky with Senan.'

Of all the benefits of going out with someone you've known since you were a teenager, she lists familiarity as the number one. 'Number two is that when I think about my future, I would love to settle back home. Home is home, you'll want to come home eventually. And it's nice to know that he feels the same, and it's not like he wants to move town. Also, we know the same people. The familiarity … for me I *like* that he's from home.'

19

Dating Apps Only Work
if You Live in a City

Tom had lived in London for a decade before he returned to the small village in County Down where he grew up, to see out lockdown from his parents' home as the pandemic began. Thirty at the time, he was ready to move out of the city anyway. He had recently gone through a divorce. Living at home with his family – his sister was also home – for the first time in years was a relief.

'It's a very small village, a very beautiful village,' he says of his home place. 'It's rural, but it doesn't feel rural in that you're literally forty minutes from Belfast, an hour from Dublin. People commute to both cities. We're isolated enough but we don't feel like it.'

Everything was in flux, the pandemic had meant his work was cancelled, but Tom is a self-starting type and immediately pivoted, beginning to get new lines of work off the ground.

When he felt ready to date again, he began to consider the apps. There was a certain amount of who-am-I-now consideration needed, he jokes. 'What's my brand persona, what's my look?' Who are you after a divorce, when you have to unexpectedly rebuild your life in a manner you never expected? Being single again, first dates, things you thought you had left forever in the past.

'Oh, those are great photos, can't really use those,' he recalls, thinking of his wedding pictures. 'It was odd, you have to kind of repackage yourself, and figure out what's going on.' The necessity to tidily package oneself into the neat shopfront self-curation required when you go on the apps is tiring.

He was very anxious about telling people he was divorced, instead of putting it on his profile, waiting until he was on a date to then mention it in person. 'I'm not saying there's a stigma about it. There were no kids, the divorce itself was really clean in that there was no money, no house involved. There was no ongoing stuff, but I was kind of anxious about people saying, oh you got divorced, why did you get divorced?'

'Dating apps only work if you live in a city,' Tom says firmly. In London, things would flow easily, from meeting on Tinder to chatting for a certain amount of time, 'until there's kind of a sweet spot where you ask somebody out. I wouldn't just ask somebody out straight away. You get to know them, flesh out some details about their profile, how was your week, how're you getting on.' He is good at dates, enjoys planning them. And in London, options were endless, logistics not a problem.

'I would always meet up with people in the afternoon. I'd plan an activity, go cycling, go to a museum, rather than just go to the pub, because that's really boring. Here in Ireland, it's like trying to arrange a space-shuttle launch. It's *so* difficult.' The dearth of people living nearby and the ensuing distance of those you might match with are problematic issues.

You begin setting your radius at around ten miles. Quickly, it's necessary to expand. Quite soon you're forty miles out (Belfast, from where Tom was living). 'A wee bit further than that, it would be Dublin. I'm so far on the east coast that I was actually picking up women on the Isle of Man.'

Suddenly you're into having to arrange accommodation for a date and it becomes 'a logistical nightmare', Tom says. 'You had to sort of wait for all the stars to align if you met somebody.' Often it would lead to pen-palling, messaging that never turns into a date – a quagmire only compounded by the restrictions of lockdown. He had a few in-person dates, in Belfast and Dublin, 'but they were so hard to engineer, especially when you're living at home with your parents,' and a couple of virtual dates in lockdown, 'sit in the house, Zoom call, couple of drinks. It was fun enough,' – a statement surely only possible because Tom is an especially chatty, engaging type. First date by Zoom sounds excruciating otherwise.

'I went through a period of being a bit depressed about it. Thinking I'm back in Ireland and I'm not going to meet anyone. I'd be going out with all my friends, it'd be the same crowd, same people, having fun, but not meeting anybody new. I stopped using dating apps. I just wasn't connecting with anybody.'

More recently, he visited Berlin for two weeks, and in contrast had three dates. 'Because it's just easier to organise. They didn't go anywhere, it's more just to get a chance to meet up and have someone show you about. They were just very pleasant, going out for a drink, a walk, stuff like that.'

At home, organisation proves much harder because of the distance between him and anyone he might date. He met a woman in another town twenty-five miles away. 'But it's an hour's drive. The number of times I said, 'oh I'll come up and see you after work. By six o'clock I'm absolutely drained. It just fizzled out. And she was really lovely.'

There's also the possibility that if you do come across someone local on the apps but aren't both swiping the right way, that can lead to moments of awkwardness. 'People who have swiped right on you and you're like no I'm not feeling it, but then you bump into them down the town. I'll be walking down the street and I'll see somebody who's liked me, but I've said no.' This happened with someone who works in a local pub.

There was a long night of the soul during the winter, the weather not helping, where he really considered whether he would remain where he was. 'I got extremely bored. I felt really lonely. I remember telling a friend, "I'm going out of my mind."'

Tom describes how he prefers meeting women in real life. The 'serendipity' of it. 'Nothing can really beat that spark across the room thing.' But he notes that the flow of new people into your life starts to dwindle as you move into your thirties. People move jobs less often, you've met all your friends' friends. The chances of meeting a person in real life become so much less likely.

Tom, in the face of losing all his work during lockdown, began several new career strands including launching a whole new business. More than that, he has really started an entirely new life. The pandemic, combined with divorce, gave him the chance to completely change his life, everything from where he lives, to his work, to his plans for the future. 'As far as my life's concerned, the pandemic was basically year zero. It gave me a chance to reset everything. My marriage broke down in the middle of 2019. Right up until then I was five years into a certain career, engaged, married, prepared to settle down.' Suddenly everything was up for reconsideration.' His work has now changed entirely from something he needed to be in London for, to something that can be done anywhere. This helped with meeting people.

Work also affords him mobility, and regular travel, which counterbalances any of the downsides of home. You get the sense he would consider settling down there long-term. 'I think where I grew up, it's not perfect, but it's quite idyllic. It was a lovely safe childhood, good schools, good resources, it never felt too far away from Dublin or London to feel too rural. It's very pretty, there's the sea there, the mountains. It's not too far away from anywhere else so I don't feel trapped.'

He bought a flat in the small town by the sea where he grew up. We speak again months later, and he's back in England for work, staying for several weeks in a city. Away from home and back in a bigger setting, he says, 'you do realise this is the stark contrast. I really miss this level of creativity. I've realised how small where I'm from is.'

He's adopted a hybrid approach to make it work for him. 'I've just bought a flat at home, I'm going to consider that my base, no matter what. It'll be my little hub. I'm invested, without feeling that I'm going to be there forever and ever. I'm going to be there, but I can go away for a couple of weeks.' He calls home his safety net, a place he knows, where he feels comfortable. 'People around me, my family nearby. And if I want to go, I can go. I'm not shackled.'

20

Somebody from Home

Emily and Connor grew up together in a border county town. As soon as adulthood allowed them to get out they both left, but they are back there now. I meet them in the house they live in with her two young children. As we talk she prepares lunch while he puts away a food shop, before collecting first one, then the second, child.

When they were growing up, Emily was in Connor's Top Three Girls. She was, in fact, his Number One, he tells me now, smiling at the memory. You get to a certain age, you start having crushes, talking about girls with your friends. There was a three-year age gap between them, so even though he 'had notions of Emily', she was largely unaware of his existence. To her, he was simply the friend of her younger brothers. At that age, a couple of years can make all the difference.

Emily's family lived out of the town, and sometimes Connor and his gang of friends would cycle the three miles out the road to see her brothers. She was rarely there. He was more likely to see her coming and going from one of the houses in town where they both had friends.

He was a geeky teenager, he recalls. Sporty, but also very studious. 'You couldn't get me away from the books.' Emily seemed like someone who was 'incredibly free. I'd be asking her about school, about whatever'. He remembers other small details, in the kitchen of a friend's house, Emily in her school uniform, 'a horrible old green convent uniform … with her thumbs stuck through the jumper', holes in the cuffs.

'I was fairly awkward and shy in those days, but I remember thinking, wow, this person has so much freedom in their mind. And how that was kind of a beautiful thing. I would have felt that I had it somewhat but wasn't there yet. I didn't have that bravery that she had at fifteen, sixteen, seventeen, I was more waiting on the world to happen rather than going after it, in the way she headed off.'

Of Connor Emily says, 'he would have been friends with my friends' brothers. And apparently he always had a crush on me. I think probably not just me,' she laughs modestly. She remembers one night when they were a bit older, being at the local disco – Oasis – housed in a large shed down the road, and he tried to kiss her. 'I pushed him away,' she smiles, 'and I remember looking back at him and thinking, what the hell? He was kind of laughing. I thought, gosh, I find him a little bit interesting now, he's a bit of craic.'

'By the time I was fifteen and ready for dancing, you were gone,' he says to her, as they move about the kitchen.

Completely by accident, Connor was there at the worst moment of her life. As seventeen-year-old Emily approached her Leaving Cert, her mother was very ill. The night before her mother died, her mother's friend came to the house to tell her there wasn't much time left. 'He [Connor] was in the room. My whole word was falling apart. I remember he said, "Can I do anything to help?" And I said, "No I just want to do this on my own." That is kind of strange, that for one of the biggest things, the most significant moments of my life, he was there.'

Connor also remembers the moment clearly. 'It was just the two of us in the living room, we were both sitting in our school uniforms. The girl who walked in ... I think went from being free, and happy, and incredibly ... you know she had this gentleness. You can't even describe it ... I think that there was a sense then that she was gone. It was like she needed to go, it was time to go. She had to sit all her exams, but I think Emily was already on her path.'

In part, it was the loss of her mother that was the catalyst for her going, Emily herself recalls. There was also, however, a sense of claustrophobia about the world she grew up in.

'My mum had just died, so I really wanted to get out of there. I also felt like I was going to maybe get stuck there.' She was the only female in the family now, and there was a lot of chat around the time that she would be staying to look after her father and younger brother.

'I just wasn't prepared to do that, I really needed to get out and start exploring the world. To get my own freedom.

I felt the confines of a very small, country world. I was eager for expansion.'

Over the years there were sporadic communications between Emily and Connor: reciprocal likes on social media, a near-miss meeting up during holidays. Connor moved abroad for work after university, settling in America. 'I think he probably forgot about me for years and got on with his life,' says Emily.

She moved to Dublin, became a fashion designer, got married and had two babies. Her marriage ended when the children were very little. 'It was like being in an accident,' she says now of the ending of the relationship. 'Even though it was coming, everything was really slow. And then that was it ... just gone.'

The tiredness in the aftermath was the worst. She moved back to her family home and her father helped her with the children. She says she was glad of the help and support at what was the hardest time of her life. After being up all night breastfeeding, she got the bus to Dublin in the morning for work. 'Going in exhausted, pumping in the toilets, rushing to get the bus back to feed the baby, putting them to the bed and just sitting there going, What, what, *what* am I going to do? Where am I going to go? Everything.' She shakes her head at how overwhelming life can be in those months after a marriage ends.

After six months she moved back to Dublin and things began to get easier. She started to feel the triumph of knowing you are keeping the show on the road. Her days were manic, but at the end of them she would often sit in the small yard of their home in one of Dublin city's oldest areas and allow herself to feel pride and delight at how she was managing. Work was going well, her kids were happy, she had childcare and a nice place to live.

'My life just fell into place, everything started to improve.' Her sense of achievement, of pride, is palpable even now, years later.

Friends told her she should get on the apps – not for her, she laughs. 'Nothing against them but it's just so not me.' She did, though, begin to consider who she would be during the times when the kids were not with her, but with their father.

'When you're so long with someone, it's a huge chunk of your life. I just couldn't even imagine what kind of person I would be,' she laughs.

'I don't know what I thought. I'd have the craic, and that would be it. And I was okay with that. It was *totally* unexpected meeting somebody. Completely unexpected.

'Connor kind of entered, suddenly he was centre stage, it was just like, *what?*' she smiles.

She sometimes feels as if she almost manifested him. She had imagined what she would need in a partner, and someone who understood where she came from was key. 'If I did meet somebody, who would they be?' she recalls thinking one day, sitting on her bed, feeding the baby. 'It would be somebody from home, whom I know, who understands, who gets what it's like to grow up here. And then about a day later he messaged saying he'd love to catch up.' Connor was going to be home for a wedding in a few months' time, and could they meet for a drink? They started texting each other on WhatsApp and chatting.

Before that, Emily had her first trip away without the kids, and it gave them time to talk more on the phone. 'It was the first time I had any time off to talk to anybody'.

Five months after he messaged, a date was planned. She almost cancelled, having had a bad afternoon. 'Then I thought, oh screw it, I'll just go and meet this guy.' It ended up being a nice date – he came back to the house where the kids were asleep upstairs with their babysitter, and they sat out in the back garden drinking wine and chatting for hours.

In the aftermath of Marian Finucane's death, her husband John Clarke gave an interview to Kathy Sheridan in the *Irish Times*. He identified the dynamic that can exist between two people in a relationship where both have been previously married. He told her that he didn't remember them having one fight in their forty years together. When his interviewer looked sceptical at that claim, Clarke said:

'See, we were both married before – and that puts manners on ya. American women say: "Always marry a married man." It's like two old mill wheels, they begin to smooth down a little, you know? I think both of us would be peacemakers rather than war-makers ... We disagreed on many things ... but I think we agreed far more often.'

How was it for her and Connor, I ask Emily?

'I was kind of crazy about him, I just found him so gorgeous, and it felt like I knew him, you know? I knew the essence of him. I think maybe that he was from home, I kind of knew who he was. Or felt like I did.'

Connor felt the same sense of certainty. 'I just knew the minute I saw her, I thought this is going to be forever,'

Connor tells me. They went for a walk down George's Street, stopped for a drink, 'just had a beautiful evening. That conversation came up, around how difficult it is, but how right this felt. It was immediate.'

Connor returned to America the following day as planned. They chatted on the phone, and two months later met again, this time in Amsterdam.

At the beginning of Covid-19, Connor decided to move home to Ireland. He had been lonely for some time in America, he says. If he wasn't working, he was on his own. So, coming home had been on the cards. 'Emily doesn't get all the credit,' he jokes. Nevertheless, if it wasn't for her, he would not have come to Ireland but would have gone somewhere else. He came to Dublin because that's where Emily was. It all just happened, they went with the flow. 'He just moved in, we didn't really discuss it,' she laughs.

'We started behaving like a couple who had been together for decades,' Connor adds. 'It's been just so incredible. She said to me one day there's absolutely no way on earth we could do this if we didn't have our childhood, and the memories that grounded us, and the trust that that brings.' Neither of them had foreseen a move back home, but for logistical reasons it became a necessity. In early 2020 they went back. We meet there, in Emily's family home, sitting around the island in the kitchen, a dog and some kittens under our feet, Emily and Connor moving about the place organising food and children. As adults, they are an almost ridiculously good-looking couple: with her dark hair, pale skin, oval face and graceful movements she looks like a classic ballerina; his has a square-jawed handsomeness.

It's strange to be back in the countryside, Emily says. They've had loads of craic motoring around in the car. She has reconnected with some friends, including the two other women who completed Connor's Top Three Girls when they were children, they both laughingly tell me. The four of them went for dinner the other night. All the same, she doesn't have especially good memories of home. 'It was hard growing up here,' she says. 'I couldn't wait to leave. So it's weird to be back. There's nothing here, it's very GAA. I liked beautiful things, the quiet, reading books. There was a cinema in town that every so often showed a quirky film, but apart from that there was nothing. And you're out in the middle of nowhere. Some of the people are hard, it's very Catholic-y. We would pray every time we were in the car, every night. And then my mum died, and I just couldn't wait to get out of here.'

Connor, arms crossed, leaning back against the range, looks over at her. 'I only came back here for Emily and my closest family,' he says. He played sports growing up, which made it easier being a teenager there, but he always knew he was going to leave.

Lockdown meant she felt their life was on pause. She doesn't drive, which compounds the frustrated feeling of being stuck. 'I'm at the mercy of others, so I have to be obliged. And I hate that because I'm so independent.'

They won't stay where they are in the long term, but they would go elsewhere in the countryside. Either way, they're building a life together. 'It's not what I thought was going to happen, at all at all ...' but then she shrugs. 'I think if we can get through this, we'll be fine. He's like a really good friend that I totally fancy.'

236

Last night they sat out in the garden after the children were asleep, having a glass of wine. 'And she said to me *how* on earth has this happened,' Connor says. 'It's all madness, but we are lucky to have found each other.' Since we talked, Emily and Connor have moved into a house of their own, a place in the middle of a forest that feels magic to them, where they live with the children and Lucky the dog.

21

A Smaller Pool of People

Paul lives in a seaside village in the south-east where he grew up. After college, he moved to Dublin for a number of years but, like so many others, came home in March 2020 when offices closed, and it became clear that we might be in this for the long haul. It's an exceptionally picturesque place, popular with tourists and people who own summer houses in the area.

As we walk through the village on our way to the beach, everyone we pass says 'hello', every car beeps a salute. 'Well, how you doing?' he nods in return. Almost the entire village will be rented out this summer, Paul says, pointing towards Main Street. Of living somewhere where everyone knows him, he says. 'I don't know any different. I have both sides. I come to Dublin and I know hardly anyone. It's good here from the perspective of if I need help, there will be always someone to give a hand if something goes wrong. I will find someone in my phone book to fix a problem. Sometimes it's a bit annoying because people want to know too much about you, but that doesn't really bother me, because I kind of keep people at arm's length as well.'

Paul's grandparents on both sides were farmers. When his paternal grandfather died, his grandmother, with small children to raise, sold the farm and moved to the place where Paul now lives. She bought the village shop so as to earn her living, placing the family at the centre of the village's life. Both Paul's parents are businesspeople: there is money in the family, but also lots of hard work. He speaks of them proudly as people who are respected, at the centre of their community, helpful neighbours. He tells me of how his mother, upon hearing of a family about to turn to moneylenders to cover funeral costs, went straight down to the funeral home to pay the bill herself. When a close family member of Paul's died, thousands of people turned up for the funeral, neighbours came to the house and organised food – the village closed down for several days.

Even though they do not plan on going into it full time, Paul and his siblings do some work for the family business. 'I knew I was never going to take over my father's business,' he tells me, 'I made that conscious decision. To give the man credit, he didn't care. There were no expectations on us to do anything.'

There is a sense of a family enterprise being carried along by a group responsibility, of various members – each with differing levels of day-to-day involvement – all invested in keeping the business going. Not all of them receive the same, if any, remuneration – an enterprise can only provide so many incomes – but each has a shared goal of carrying this concern through to the next generation. Paul and his brother discuss what his niece, currently the only grand-child, will inherit from their generation, planning how they will manage it. Paul himself won't have children. 'I don't want to own a child,' he says, then roars with laughter at what he has said. Proves his point, he grins.

Paul is tall and strapping, funny and bright. He's excellent company: sarcastic, but underneath it a layer of kindness. He answers any question with extreme honesty: when I ask him if he talks to his mother about who he's dating, he laughs and says no. 'I wouldn't really, because it's so crude – it's not the kind of thing that you'd talk to your mother about. And I don't have a filter. If you ask me a very direct question, I'll give you a *very* direct answer.'

Now aged twenty-nine, he was born a year before the decriminalisation of sex acts between men in 1993. When I ask what age he was when he realised he was gay, he says he doesn't recall.

'I don't have the answer to that. And that's not being smart, I'd tell you straight out, I'm quite open. I would have been interested in cooking and gardening, and all the clas-sic things that homosexual men are into. All my cousins would be very interested in machinery, and I wasn't.'

He can see, looking back, that his was an idyllic child-hood. In the holidays and at weekends his mother would throw them out of the house at nine o'clock, entire days would be spent down the fields, Paul leading the pack of siblings, cousins and friends.

Independence and finance are priorities. He started various business enterprises when he was twelve, which made him money. Of friends he says, 'I would have met them whenever I wanted, but it was always on my terms. I didn't give a hoot. I wasn't that person who needed to meet people every day.'

No one ever teased him as a child, 'because I was always as tough as nails. I'd like to see someone take me on, because I would have them for breakfast' – he means verbally, not physically. He has a sharp tongue when he wants to. He knew he was gay, but it didn't become a focus in his life until the end of college. 'I suppose you think, fuck it – I'd better do something about this before I end up a lonely old spinster.'

His first kiss with a man was in his first year of college, but there were no boyfriends. 'Fuck buddies maybe, but it was never anything serious. Gay men, basically they'd sleep with anyone. If you're out and you're drunk, you're going to end up sleeping with someone if you want to. You would have started off just riding but then it would evolve into a friendship and so to a point you would have been dating them. Well not really, like. I could have been off with someone else.'

Paul is a planner. His job involves financial assessment, and he brings the same analytical gaze to his own life. He decided he didn't want to get tied to someone in college who came from another part of Ireland – what was the future in that?

'In college you might have had frivolous relationships, but I knew I might end up in Dublin, they might end up in New York, so what's the point in pouring energy, and emotional energy, into something when you're going to throw it in the bin in a few years' time? And the drama of that then. No, fuck that.'

After college he did move to Dublin, and within six months was in a serious relationship with a man he met on Grindr.

Paul describes the instant gratification available to him on the apps. 'Let's say I wanted to have sex tonight: I'd go on an app and get the ride later. You could be quite open about it. One of you will invariably get to the point. *Do you want to have fun? What has you on this?*'

'Oh, they're a cesspit,' he continues. 'It's a thing you'd never want your child to be involved in, to be honest with you. I'm not an angel, I'm no shrinking violet I can tell you, but those things are vile. It walks off me, I'd be like, pfft, fucking eejits. But … they're not the kind of thing you'd want to be involved with for the rest of your life.'

His last relationship ended two years before we talk, and he has been on Grindr ever since. It's beginning to wear him down. 'It's like, this is boring,' he sighs. 'Sex is a laugh. Being on the dating scene, having casual relation-ships, it can be fun. But it can also become soul-destroying. You may build up a relationship in terms of a friendship to a point with someone, but you're never going to go from being that kind of acquaintance to a boyfriend, because you know it's just sex. You know you're not going to fall in love with them. Because you're not going to leave that side down.'

Why not, I wonder?

'If you're just meeting someone for the ride, and if you know it's just for the ride, why bother getting emotionally involved? Because you'll get hurt. If gay men don't figure this out, they are in for a horrible time as they will have their heart broken many times.'

It focuses you, he reflects on the grimmer side of dating apps. He's had enough, and now wants a relationship. 'Now I'm at the point where I want to have a relationship with one person – you're trying to sift out the bastards from the whatever, like.'

Paul has been home now for almost two years. He is unconvinced there are any major distinctions, beyond what one might term logistical, between using Grindr in an urban or rural setting.

'I don't think geography really comes into this. People who say, oh it makes such a difference – the only reason it makes a difference in the country is because there's less of a concentration of people. It's the same as anything. There's a smaller pool of people to choose from. It's like going to buy a house in Dublin. There are more houses available. Are they what you want? Maybe, maybe not. Are they what you can afford? Maybe, maybe not. It's a similar situation in my eyes. It's just a smaller pool. The sheer volume of people that are gay in a rural area is less.'

Every Friday evening, the grid on his app lights up – a reflection of the area's popularity with tourists and second homeowners – as an influx of weekenders arrives. This area is very, very hot for tourists,' he says. On occasion, he will see married men he knows locally on Grindr. 'One of the big differences at home is that there'd be a lot of older people. It's because gay men didn't come out in rural areas until they were a lot older. A lot of young people leave the country to go to the city to get good jobs. The older married lads are brazen as hell,' he adds with a laugh.

His own situation is that he's out, with reservations. 'I suppose I would be very reserved about it myself,' he says when I ask if he has come out to his family and neighbours. 'It's very much none of anyone's business. I know someone in the area and he was pretending to be straight when he was gayer than the pink pound. But he just came out naturally. He moved somebody into his house, which was quite courageous. He kind of kept it under wraps for a while, but I got to know his partner through Grindr.'

In his article 'Sexual citizenship: rhetoric or reality for rural gay men in Ireland and England?' (www.tandfonline.com), Aidan McKearney describes how his research showed that 'rural cultures and spaces can be doggedly masculine', with traditional concepts of masculinity dominating and 'setting the tone for how rural men should be, with images of rural masculinity emphasising ruggedness, physical strength, macho individualism, and emotional independence'.

I wonder if traditional definitions of masculinity make it hard for Paul to come out fully. He seems to acknowledge that it might, to some extent, inhibit his ability to do some of the work he undertakes for the family business. 'To a point, but I think within my own right, I'm quite a strong person. My persona changes if I'm in bad form with someone, over owing a debt, or not doing their job. I'm not saying I'm a maaaaaan, as in I'm never going to be one of those GAA heads down the village drinking pints,' he smiles.

Part of his work for his father's business involves the finances of the business.

'By its very nature that's a tough thing to do. If you're going into a farmer's yard, and some of them are obnoxious bastards, they could throw the whole thing at you, "shut up you pouf". I've never seen it, and without coming across as obnoxious, I don't think they would say it to me. Because number one, they might have too much respect for my family. Number two, they're probably afraid of me giving out to them. Because there's two versions of me, there's work Paul and social Paul.'

Fear around inheritance might be an issue for people coming out, he reflects. 'I can't put words into other people's mouths, but my gut feeling is people still have this fear that if they are openly gay, they might lose their patch. To a point I was probably a bit like that myself. I didn't care about my father's business, it's so stressful. Business can be difficult in rural Ireland, especially around payment. But there are certain things my parents would have, that I would like to get,' he says, laughing. 'And for a while I was like, oh Jesus, what if I don't produce 3.5 children, and have a car and go to the country market on a Saturday morning for my fucking vegetables, I'm not going to get x and x. And then I was like, fuck it, who cares? It's my life and not their life, like it or lump it kind of thing. I've also come to realise I am clever enough to make it on my own without handouts.'

'I no longer have to worry a whole lot about money, as I should be grand,' he adds. 'I think that has made me far more relaxed. When I was on a small salary it stressed me as when you're gay, especially when you're dating or having fun with older guys, you see the wealth and you don't want to be the gay with little, as they are usually living in terrible conditions and that's scary for me.'

Living where he is, there is no nearby strong visible gay network or scene. It makes the apps more important. For the most part, they are the only way of getting to know other gay men. As you get to know a few, you do get to know more organically, Paul says.

The first time we meet, when I ask if his father knows he's gay, he demurs. 'Emmmm, well he does and he doesn't.' Would he ever discuss it with him? 'No. No, no, no, no.' Then towards the end of our time together, he casually drops in that he's 'kind of half seeing a guy now for the last while. And it probably will manifest into something more'.

They met on Grindr. We meet again months later, and during laps of his local beach Paul updates me on the man who has now been upgraded to boyfriend. They're texting a lot and have met up a few times. It will change what he said before about discussing his relationship status with his father.

'It's gonna change, it's gonna change a lot now,' he smiles. 'Because I'm with someone now.'

Before, going into things too much with his family felt like unnecessary fuss. 'I never saw the value – this is just my black-and-white personality – in causing a whole load of drama for no reason.' It's not that they don't know, they just don't talk about it much.

'You can come out but don't come out too far,' McKearney recorded one of his interviewees as commenting in his article examining Sexual Citizenship. For Paul, the difference is one of both the seriousness of a relationship but also the nature of that person. Unlike in the past, now he has found someone who understands the values of the place and the people where he is from.

'I was with other people in the past for three or four years, but I could never be bothered introducing them because I knew they wouldn't integrate into the family.' This was nothing to do with sexuality, but shared values. His boyfriend now is also from the countryside and comes from a similar background of business and farming.

'My ex-boyfriend just wouldn't work in our house, because if somebody needs help, it doesn't matter if it's money or time, my parents would be very generous. It wasn't that he wasn't generous, but he couldn't understand that if someone rang my parents and they were in trouble, they would be straight there. In our house, everyone kind of slobs around, you come in, if you want a cup of tea you can make it yourself, if we're having dinner, you take what you're given. I don't want someone to be in my family who is not going to have the same kind of values as we would have. They have to fit within your wider family.'

Since we last spoke, Paul has deleted Grindr. He and his boyfriend have had the exclusivity conversation, a relationship status that *cannot* be assumed in online dating, I learn. 'If I wanted to go and get the ride now, I could set up a profile. It's like anything, if you have something in your hands, there's a temptation there. You have to decide: one or the other. If you're going to be serious with someone it needs to be spoken about, and it needs to be a fair conversation. I think if you don't foster a fair package or set of rules, that's where gay men fall down. They don't speak about it, but I know loads of gay men who are cheating on their partners. It's so normal.'

In accordance with what he describes as his old-fashioned principles – black and white – there has to be a sense of mutual respect. 'You have to tell the truth, have to be fair.' He has found a man who is in accordance with this way of being, this mindset.

We're walking back from the beach to the village when we pass people struggling with the gates of a hotel. They don't have the keypad password. Paul dashes across to help the strangers, rings the front desk, knows the manager, gets them sorted.

He jogs back across the road to where I'm waiting for him, looks back at the beach, takes in the wide sweep of the road, surrounded on both sides by forest. 'I would happily live here for the rest of my life,' he tells me.

Conclusion

I wrote this book during a pandemic, beginning research in late 2020 and completing it in the summer of 2022. It seems like a funny time to be writing something that is all about how people connect, given the locked-down, restricted circumstances we were living under at intervals, and I was concerned that my research might give an unreal snapshot of the story I was trying to tell, one only relevant to life during a pandemic.

'How did the pandemic affect dating?' I was often asked by those who knew I was working on this project. As it happened, not as much as I feared. In part, this is because of how many of these stories are told, not just a short snapshot in someone's life, but a deep dive into their past, beyond the period during which this book was being written. These are in many cases stories that capture a culmination of, rather than a 'live', moment. But more than that, the pandemic did not have as strong an impact on how people meet each other in rural places. This is because the Covid-19-era changes to socialising in urban areas were already part of the rural experience. Longer time periods between beginning to talk to someone online and meeting up are a given when you're both living in different counties and not in the same city. The simple logistics were already an issue. Dates that don't revolve around the pub but rather the outdoors were more likely to be an option in the countryside anyway.

There is also the fact that the pandemic had a positive impact on the possibilities of rural living. The ability to work from home, where before such a request might have been summarily turned down, meant that for many people, returning to live in the place where they grew up or fulfilling a long-held but assumed-impossible dream of abandoning city life, became an option for the first time. Migration patterns have reversed somewhat – who is to say with what longevity? – but it seems fair to wonder whether the pandemic might have a long-term rejuvenating impact on rural Ireland. In light of this, the means and methods of how we meet a partner and the ways of life looked at in this book are now relevant for so many more people.

With many people I spoke to for this book, the meanings of place were manifold. There was the fact that their place provided them with a way of life that was specific to it. That could be a slow pace of living, affordability, the connections of family and those they grew up with, a sense of refuge, of safety, a type of work, the ability to buy a home, or a sense of balance between work and other things in their life.

When it came to finding a partner, often the priority was meeting a person who had a similar appreciation for and understanding of their place: a farmer who needed someone to comprehend the demands of running a farm; someone who had chosen an especially isolated community in which to live, who needed someone who would also appreciate that way of life. Place could be the deciding factor in two people coming together. It could also be the thing that meant a person would stay single: I will live in this tiny community because it is my home, even though I know it will make it that much harder to find someone.

Two things came up again and again in my conversations. Lifestyle, and the phrase 'back on the apps', the latter invariably said with a sigh and a slight shrug to denote effort. Lifestyle was the kind of life that the place they were in – whether they had grown up there or come to it in adulthood – offered them. Going back on the apps meant that after yet another break they were, reluctantly, going back to online dating, despairing at the prospect of the often-bruising experience but determined to meet someone.

Sometimes, the two urges would collide and prove mutually exclusive: primacy of place over longing for love. Sometimes, one complemented the other: finding a person who shared their love of a specific way of life offered by a place was the guiding factor in finding a partner.

While life in lockdown did push us to live more online that we might otherwise have done, I don't know that it will have a long-lasting effect on how we meet people now that restrictions have lifted. What it might do is change in the long term *where* we date. Traditional internal migration patterns have been from the rural to the urban, but the pandemic has allowed people to live their life in places they might otherwise never have dreamed of. Some have returned to their hometown, or to a rural community so much more affordable than the city they previously lived in.

Much of what people are referring to when they extol the virtues of their place is their community. The network of people they have found that sustains them and the importance of that to them, sometimes to the point where they will prioritise it over the search for a partner. The wave of movement caused by the pandemic means rural communities are now an option as they were not previously. The question of what result this will have on the search for love in smaller communities is fascinating.

Acknowledgements

This book was the idea of Aoife K. Walsh, commissioning editor at New Island. I would like to thank her for the immense care and attention to detail she brought to every aspect of its creation, from early Zooms, brainstorming over the contents, through to considering every detail of the cover.

My thanks to my editor at New Island, Djinn von Noorden. Especially with a book that is telling the stories of so many real people's lives, and the responsibility that that involves, having an editor whose judgement you instantly trust completely is hugely helpful.

Thank you to Caoimhe Fox and Deirdre Roberts for their huge effort and enthusiasm in getting this book out into the world; to Stephen Reid for proofreading and to Allan J. Crann for the legal read.

And to everyone else at New Island, Edwin Higel, Mariel Deegan, Mary Deegan and Djamel White, for all their work.

Thanks to my agent, Sallyanne Sweeney, and the team at MMBcreative.

To Holly Pereira for creating the most beautiful cover. Emily Hourican, who suggested me for this project, as always, a true supporter of others. To Yvonne Hogan and Mary O'Sullivan for endless steers, advice and professional support. To my editor, Leslie Ann Horgan, whose professional support enabled me to work on this project, and to all my colleagues at the *Sunday Independent*.

To Cassie Delaney and Aisling Keenan for *rogue*-related matters and much more. Rachel Lysaght for being the greatest sounding board.

To Seán and Dympna Smyth, for the use of the most peaceful of homes in which to get the first draft over the line.

I spoke to many people over almost two years in researching this book, my sincere apologies if I have left your name off this list. Huge thanks to Dr Nicola Fox Hamilton for her fascinating insights about online dating.

To Lucy Rand, Mairead Loughman, Hugh Redmond, Frances Kelleher, Gabriela Meade Diaz, Gordon Peppard, Chloe Murphy, Dr Richard Butler, Aisling Molloy, Sarah Phillips, Daniel Buckley, Naadia Ibrahim, Sharon Nolan, Ejiro Ogbevoen, Orla Diffily, Joanne Mangan, Noel Clancy, Rebecca Ryan and Maureen McLaughlin from the Irish Countrywoman's Association, the many Macra branches who helped with information and interviewees, Ella McSweeney, Feargal Harrington, Emma Blain, Eithne Buckley, Niall Doorhy, Grace Alice O'Shea.

Sophie White, for endless steers and advice. Emer Black, Ciarán Hynes, Daragh Black Hynes and Song Yue for their never-ending support of Sarah and me, which enabled all the travel involved in this book. To Sarah, for cover conversations, endless interest in how books are created, and general all-round inspiration.

And thanks to Kevin Smyth, for support that included everything from the most practical, to historical, geographical and architectural steers, to endless, *endless* conversations about how to tell the stories in this book.

And to the all people who shared their stories in their book, my sincere gratitude.